PRAISE FOR *BUILDING THE FIT ORGANIZATION*

"Dan Markovitz is a remarkable sensei, and this book reflects his ability to take complex content and make it digestible and actionable. Dan makes us realize that lean is not a mystery that migrated from Japan but skills that anyone can master regardless of their industry or line of work. This book should encourage readers to use lean thinking at work and in their personal life."

—Sherry Neubert, Chief Information Officer, Goodyear Tire & Rubber Company

"In writing *Building the Fit Organization*, Dan Markovitz explains what it takes to become a successful Lean Organization without using any of the Lean jargon . . . making the subject more understandable and approachable. And in doing so, he demonstrates that *any* organization, not just manufacturing, can become Fit. For executives that have avoided the subject until now, or those who have tried and struggled with it, *Building the Fit Organization* is required reading."

—Orry Fiume, Vice President Finance–Retired, The Wiremold Company, and coauthor, *Real Numbers: Management Accounting in a Lean Organization*

"The best time to plant a tree is 20 years ago . . . so too with starting the journey to organizational fitness. The second best time is *today*. *Building the Fit Organization* shows you how, with specific first steps for next Monday morning. Thanks Dan Markovitz for sharing your wisdom. Whether personally or organizationally, you remind us that there is always room for improvement."

—Rich Sheridan, CEO, Chief Storyteller, Menlo Innovations, Author, *Joy, Inc.: How We Built a Workplace People Love.*

"What do physical fitness and organizational fitness have in common? More than you think. Dan Markovitz's ability to help you think in different ways about your organization makes *Building the Fit Organization* a must-read for all leaders."

—Helen Zak, President and COO, ThedaCare Center for Healthcare Value

"Dan Markovitz continues his enduring quest to help organizations, leaders, and people to contribute more with less, to improve effectiveness not just efficiency, to increase achievement and enjoyment. He is a writer of noble intent, making an impact through the hard discipline of writing well."

—Jim Collins, author, *Good to Great*, *Built to Last*, and *Great by Choice*

"Dan is right: this book is not about running, and it is not about Toyota improvement methods. Nonetheless, the book shows how you can become a better runner if you follow a few principles, and how a company can improve by following those same principles. Dan has a remarkable talent in making things simple and proving that companies may already know most of what is needed to improve. No copying of Toyota concepts, no strange terms or ideas—just a little learning, hard work, and good coaching."

—Norbert Majerus, Lean champion at The Goodyear Tire and Rubber Company and author of *Lean-Driven Innovation*

"Dan Markovitz uses the fitness metaphor to provide great practical insights on lean transformation. The book is full of good thinking punctuated by thought-provoking examples."

—Peter Ward, Co-Director, Center for Operational Excellence, Fisher College of Business

"(Dan) does a fantastic job of presenting both the theory and the practical applications critical for moving toward being a fit company. His approach is direct and easily translated into actionable items for today's business leader. As I read the book I found myself constantly making lists of actions that I later shared with my team so we could become a more fit organization."

—Brian Thompson, General Manager, ExOfficio

"Outstanding performance is the goal. Organizational health is the means. And fitness is at the core of it all. Markovitz is spot-on regarding his observations and recommendations for building a fit organization that thrills customers, thrives during difficult times, and provides a meaningful work environment for the employees who deserve nothing less."

—Karen Martin, President, The Karen Martin Group, author, *The Outstanding Organization*

"Dan is one of today's leading voices revealing the role of skill development in organizations, and how practice is a vital ingredient for acquiring new skill, mindset and making change really happen."

—Mike Rother, author of *Toyota Kata*

"Dan has done it again with *Building the Fit Organization*. He has identified the essential shift and plan needed to create a fit organization. He has created the perfect analogy of linking the trifecta of key elements for creating a true Lean Enterprise Transformation (People, Process, and Purpose) to a successful physical fitness plan. He identifies the key attributes in Process with the necessary horizontal flow and leader standard work. He defines the need for Servant Leadership and extensive coaching at all levels with the organization's most valuable asset, its People. He then draws the work out plan to cover an organization's Purpose with practical tools and elements for operational excellence and truly achieving the organization's purpose. A must-read for all athletes of performance improvement."

—John M. Rubio, Vice President, Simpler NA/Truven Health Analytics

"Dan brings to life the essence of a successful continuous improvement journey—it is all about the people. By reframing the journey as a quest for organizational fitness, Dan captures practical, profound insights that will drive any aspiring Lean organization to greater success."

—Bob Chapman, CEO, Barry-Wehmiller

BUILDING THE
FIT
ORGANIZATION

**Six Core Principles for Making Your Company
Stronger, Faster, and More Competitive**

Daniel Markovitz

Mc
Graw
Hill
Education

New York Chicago San Francisco Athens London Madrid
Mexico City Milan New Delhi Singapore Sydney Toronto

1 2 3 4 5 6 7 8 9 0 QFR/QFR 1 2 1 0 9 8 7 6 5

ISBN   978-1-259-58717-7
MHID   1-259-58717-7

e-ISBN   978-1-259-58718-4
e-MHID   1-259-58718-5

McGraw-Hill Education books are available at special quantity discounts to use as premiums and sales promotions, or for use in corporate training programs. To contact a representative, please visit the Contact Us page at www.mhprofessional.com.

Contents

Acknowledgments

Some books spring full-grown from the author's forehead, like Athena from Zeus. This book was not one of them. I am indebted to many people for their help in making this book possible.

Beau Keyte (abetted by two bottles of Tempranillo at dinner one cold night in Toronto) inspired this journey in the first place. Not only did he convince me that I could write a book about improvement without revisiting the well-trod turf of Toyota, he convinced me that it would actually be interesting and valuable. And Beau knows.

Jorrit De Groot, Carolyn Brodsky, Ed Schmults, Bryan Crowell, Ted Makros, Jeff Schox, Will Blount, Young Joen, Larry Barrett, Scott Tuchel, Wim de Jager, Marlena Kane, James Hereford, Rich Sheridan, Steve Brenneman, Joe Swartz, Brian Wellinghoff, Roger Morgan, Jerry Pomije, Nick Graham, and Kimberly Brown—you have my gratitude for inviting me into your workplaces, for being so generous with your time and so willing to share your stories with me. What you're doing in your organizations inspires me, and I hope will inspire others.

Ron Pereira, Mark Graban, and Bill Waddell provided important introductions that smoothed the way in my research. Thank you for making my work so much easier and saving me enormous amounts of time.

Finally, my deepest thanks go to Tom Ehrenfeld, who saw what this book could be before I did, and whose ability to push me into deeper intellectual waters still makes me shake my head in wonder.

BUILDING THE
FIT
ORGANIZATION

Introduction

Three laps on my school's beat-up cinder track—a mere three-quarters of a mile—was as far as I could run without stopping in eighth grade. I had never done any sports in school before—sports were not exactly a big part of the curriculum in my previous school, an orthodox yeshiva—and I struggled with asthma and allergies. In ninth grade I joined the cross-country team, and while I could run the full race distance of 2.5 miles without stopping, I was dead last in every race. But I kept training, working on my form, my stamina, and my speed. By my senior year, I was undefeated in the two-mile on the track, and I continued on to reasonable success in college and beyond. I was no all-American, mind you, but I did pretty well for a guy who started out as far in the back as I did. In later years I coached high school cross-country runners, working with some very talented kids, as well as some who were just like I had been.

No, you haven't mistakenly bought the wrong book: this isn't a book about my running career. It's about business, and specifically, about how organizations can become fitter, stronger, faster, and more competitive. But understanding my background helps explain my unique perspective on the long, competitive race that organizations find themselves in today.

Over the past 20 years, American businesses have learned a great deal about the Toyota Production System. This system, also called lean, has led Toyota to become one of the most successful and admired companies in the world in a comparatively short time. The benefits of applying lean manufacturing principles to any kind of organization are well known by this point: greater profitability, higher quality, lower costs, and improved employee engagement, to name just a few.

And yet, despite the prevalence of business books that analyze and explain how the Toyota Production System works, the number of organizations that have actually achieved a lean transformation, or even maintained a commitment to continuous improvement, is vanishingly small. Most organizations abandon their efforts midstream or, daunted by the challenges of understanding lean concepts, don't even attempt to adapt and adopt the lessons from Toyota to their own businesses.

The reasons for this failure are varied. Management in some companies can't make the intellectual leap needed to translate a system from auto manufacturing to, say, healthcare or banking. In other firms the jargon—*heijunka, kanban, muda*, 5S, water spiders, even the very term *lean*—is too high a hurdle for people to overcome, so lean is never seen as anything other than an alien way of thinking and working. Still other firms make operational improvements, but they prove ephemeral, lasting only as long as the leadership team is intact or as long as business results are positive. Performance eventually regresses to the mean, and top management shifts its focus to something else. And of course, many other companies don't even try to improve operations: people are too busy doing their regular jobs and trying to hit their month-end numbers to even think about adding improvement work to their daily responsibilities.

There's one other factor that hinders companies from following the path of operational excellence blazed by Toyota: they're worshipping at the church of Toyota.

This assertion is heretical. Toyota is the exemplar of operational excellence. It's the company that has taken the embryonic ideas at the core of lean manufacturing and brought them to full flower. It's the most profitable automaker in the world. Who better to look to as a model?

Indeed, legions of companies around the world make pilgrimages to the head office in Japan to learn Toyota's secrets. They purchase books by the score on the "Toyota Way" as it applies to leadership, culture, healthcare, product development, and pretty much any other field you care to name. They deploy phalanxes of Lean Six Sigma Master Black Belts (along with a host of other colored belts) throughout their organizations. Yet they still prove unable to copy Toyota's way to success.

I want to suggest that their efforts fail precisely *because* they're trying to copy Toyota—which is why this book doesn't even mention Toyota. (Actually, I mention Toyota three times: One is in a quote by a journalist, and the other two times I needed to identify speakers who worked there.) An average company trying to copy Toyota is like a couch potato who wants to start running, copying the training regimen of Haile Gebrselassie, one of the greatest distance runners in history, who set 22 world records in the 5,000 meters, 10,000 meters, and marathon during the course of his magnificent career. Good luck with that. Or like a weekend Hamptons vacationer following the swimming program of Michael Phelps, who won 18 Olympic gold medals. Those athletes are so inconceivably advanced that attempting to crib their training routine would inevitably lead to injury, frustration, and failure. It's pointless to even look at how they train if you can't even run a mile or swim a lap in a pool.

Rather than slavishly copying Gebrselassie or Phelps, the pursuit of physical fitness or athletic excellence rests upon the following:

- Defining a goal (winning the gold medal, running a four-hour marathon, or breaking 100 on a golf course)
- Knowing what skills are required to reach that goal
- Acquiring those skills through coaching and practice
- Choosing the right performance metrics to evaluate progress

THE FIT ORGANIZATION

The corporate landscape is littered with the carcasses of organizations that have failed in their pursuit of the Toyota Way. It's clear that trying to *be like* Toyota is a mistake. What leaders need to do instead is *learn from* Toyota—learn how to convert their flabby organizations into "fit" ones. A fit organization, in my view, is a dynamic, constantly improving, profoundly customer-focused entity that delivers superior performance and results over the long haul. Becoming that kind of organization rests upon:

Making an unshakeable *commitment* to
Increase value provided by
Doing the *right work* (things that deliver value to the customer)
In the *right way* (through standard work)
With *continuous monitoring* of processes (through visual management systems)
And *structured coaching* for everyone (using the scientific method)

Not surprisingly, these are the themes of the six chapters of this book.

My goal is to teach you how to build—and lead—a "fit" company. I've attempted to distill the critical principles from Toyota's lean playbook and couch these concepts in everyday business language, free from Japanese and English jargon. Henceforth, I won't even use the word *lean*. To make these principles even more understandable, I've grounded them in an extended analogy of physical fitness and athletic excellence, something that most people have some experience with. Throughout the book, I draw parallels between the critical principles for business "fitness" and the principles for physical fitness—because the same concepts that make for a fit person make for a fit company.

To be clear, none of the companies I use as case studies have attained Toyota's stratospheric level of excellence, but that's precisely why they're better exemplars than the auto giant: these companies are understandable, reachable. They may not implement all the principles, all the time, in all parts of their organizations, but they do it in some areas, and as a result they've become fitter and more profitable. The companies portrayed here are inspiring because they're just like us—only a little better, a little fitter.

You can be, too.

THE MACHINE THAT CHANGED THE WORLD

In 1990, researchers James Womack, Daniel Jones, and Daniel Roos published *The Machine That Changed the World*. The book was a lengthy academic analysis of the operational and performance differences between General Motors and Toyota. In many respects, it became the book that changed the world. (It also changed my world: it was the first time I had heard of lean and the Toyota Production System, and it led me on a journey to learn more about it that continues today.) For the first time, American auto manufacturers could see just how much better Toyota was than they were. The numbers were astonishing.

To be sure, there were companies that had been to Japan to study and learn from Toyota prior to the book's publication. For that matter, Toyota itself had started a joint venture with GM in the United States in 1984, and Honda opened its first U.S. plant in 1982. And people like W. Edwards Deming had been preaching for decades about the need to change and improve. But *The Machine That Changed the World* provided not only the hard evidence that there was a better way—a much, much, much better way—to manufacture products, but it showed how Toyota did it.

Perhaps more important, the book raised awareness of this new approach to operations and production outside of the narrow confines of the auto industry. In the quarter century since its publication, knowledge of, and interest in, lean manufacturing has spread. Countless manufacturing firms have developed their own versions of the Toyota Production System, and the principles have been adapted and adopted in other fields as diverse as healthcare, banking, retail, and even government (hard to believe, but true). The truth is that whether you're producing healthy patients, completed mortgage applications, or driver's licenses, the same fundamental concepts apply:

> Make an unshakeable *commitment* to
> *Increase value* provided by
> Doing the *right work*
> In the *right way*
> With *continuous monitoring* of processes
> And *structured coaching* for everyone.

These ideas may be simple, but they're not so easy to implement. I know that. But as a business consultant, a former competitive runner, and a coach, I also know that changing the context and the language used to explain an idea can make all the difference. My hope is that by placing these principles in the relatively familiar, jargon-free context of athletic excellence and physical fitness, you'll be able to grasp the concepts more easily and be able to explain them in a more compelling manner to your team.

If you can do that, you'll take the first steps down the road toward organizational fitness.

1

Commit to Improvement

Fit leaders (and fit companies) didn't get that way by accident. They're fit on purpose. They mindfully and intentionally pursue a well-defined course of action that makes them stronger, faster, and more agile over the long run. Fit companies love problems because they're high-leverage opportunities for improvement. They engage in rigorous, scientific thinking at all levels of the organization to analyze and solve problems. They create a blame-free culture by focusing on the systems and processes that aren't operating at the desired level rather than on the people who work in those systems. In so doing, they eliminate the fear that shackles employee creativity and liberate employees to close the gaps between where they are today and where they want to be tomorrow.

Don't try to find a spot on the StairMaster or in the spin class on January 8. The busiest week of the year at a gym is the second week of the new year. Fueled by an excess of calories from too much food and drink during the holiday season, people make resolutions to lose weight, work out, and get fit. The gym is packed as tightly as people are packed into their spandex. Of course, by February the gym is back to normal. Most people predictably abandon their resolutions in short order—they're bored, they're busy, they're sick, they're tired. Life gets in the way. They lack the commitment (or know-how) to sustain their fitness initiative, and the next thing you know, they're anxiously searching for diet and fitness tips to wriggle into their bathing suits for the summer.

Organizations aren't so different from individuals. Preceding the new fiscal year, the management team announces its goal to capture the top spot in the marketplace, rolls out 37 new strategic initiatives, and vows to elevate employee engagement and make the organization a great place to work. By the second quarter, it's business as usual. Organizations get caught up in trying to make the monthly or quarterly numbers, departments are overwhelmed by the multitude of new (and often contradictory) initiatives for which they lack the people or resources, and employees feel no more connection to the company's leadership and vision than they did before. The organization loses momentum on its initiatives, often fails to achieve its stated goals, and waddles along until the next annual strategic off-site, whereupon the cycle repeats itself.

For both the individual and the organization, the problem is the same. There may be a stated goal—lose 15 pounds, improve muscle tone—but there's often no clearly defined program to reach that fitness goal. Or even if there is a program, it may simply be a fad that promises huge results with minimal effort: think vibrating belts, ThighMaster, 8 Minute Abs, and the latest diet pills. More significantly, for the people who abandon their fitness efforts, going to the gym and exercising is something that's external to the daily flow of their lives. It's a chore that requires additional time and commitment, not something that's as fundamental and core to their lives as, say, going to work, or playing with their kids, or even brushing their teeth.

In the same way, most organizations have annual goals—take the top spot in the market, lift employee engagement—but they lack clearly defined improvement programs to reach their goals. As with individuals, there is no end to the number of business fads that promise to get companies to the promised land—emotional intelligence, Six Sigma, business process reengineering, management by walking around (MBWA), and so on. But efforts to achieve those goals are episodic (at best) or sporadic (at worst), because they're not seen as integral to the organization's daily operations. They're made "when we have some free time," or before the boss asks about them at the quarterly performance review.

Truly fit individuals don't so much make a generic commitment to exercise as they weave exercise and health into the daily fabric of their lives. Similarly, truly fit organizations don't so much make a commitment to an improvement "program" per se as they build improvement into the way they operate on an ongoing basis, every day.

The Improvement Imperative

In a 2014 *New Yorker* article, James Surowiecki makes the case that the biggest change in performance over the past few decades isn't so much that the best performers are so much better than they used to be—although they are—but rather that so many people in these fields are so extraordinarily good:

> In the nineteen-seventies, there were only two chess players who had Elo ratings (a measure of skill level) higher than 2700. These days, there are typically more than thirty such players. Analyses of great players' games from even thirty years ago uncover moves that, by today's standards, are clear blunders. . . . The quality of classical musicians has improved dramatically as well, to the point that virtuosos are now, as the *Times* music critic Anthony Tommasini has observed of pianists, "a dime a dozen." . . . James Conlon, the conductor of the Los Angeles Opera, has said, "The professional standards are higher everywhere in the world compared to twenty or forty years ago." Pieces that were once considered too difficult for any but the very best musicians are now routinely played by conservatory students.[1]

It's not just chess and music, either. The story is the same for professional athletes. Innate athletic ability is now the bare minimum requirement for athletes. It's a starting point, nothing more. What really matters is a relentless, focused commitment to practice and improvement. Gone are the days when professional baseball and football players sold insurance or laid bricks in the off-season and came to training camp to get in shape. Today's pro athletes spend the off-season developing new skills and honing their physical condition. At the highest levels, there really is no off-season, only a different training focus. An athlete who isn't willing to embrace that commitment to fitness and improvement, to weave it into the warp and weft of his or her life, isn't going to compete at that level for very long.

The business world has seen the same shift. In the decades after World War II, American manufacturers bestrode the world like colossuses, unchallenged by foreign competitors. With dominance came complacency in the form of low productivity and poor quality. One study, in 1969, found that a third of the people who bought a new American car judged it to be in unsatisfactory condition when it was delivered. In 1974, service calls for American color televisions were five times as common as for Japanese televisions, and in 1979 it took American companies more than three times longer to manufacture their sets.[2]

The imperative to improve became unavoidable with the arrival of foreign competition, primarily in the form of Japanese manufacturers that had absorbed the quality lessons of W. Edwards Deming. For some companies and some industries, it was too late: the American television industry, which had more than 90 manufacturers in the 1950s, ceased to exist in any meaningful way when Zenith, the last American-owned television manufacturer, was sold to Korea's LG Electronics in 1995.[3] By contrast, the U.S. auto industry has survived, but only by dramatically improving product quality. As in sports and music, however, the gap between the best and the worst in the industry has shrunk. In 1998, J.D. Power and Associates found that the most reliable car had 92 problems per 100 vehicles, while the least reliable had 517, a gap of 425. In 2012 the gap had closed to 284 problems. As Dave Sargent, automotive vice president with J.D. Power says, "We don't have total clunkers like we used to."[4] And it's not just cars: despite increasing complexity in nearly every product category you can think of, quality and reliability has only increased—think cell phones, airplanes, TVs, and computers. The lesson is clear: improve or face extinction.

Over the past half century, training methods in all sports have changed and improved. Fitness is no longer just about lifting heavy weights in the gym or practicing in the Texas summer heat without drinking water. The same is true in organizational improvement. The techniques for improvement have themselves developed and changed since 1950, and that's been a huge factor in the productivity gains of the past decades. It's not worth getting into a lengthy disquisition on the ways in which these methods have changed. Suffice it to say that by now, there are proven methods and mindsets that make the practice of improvement teachable and doable:

> Make an unshakable *commitment* to
> *Increase value* provided by
> Doing the *right work* (things that deliver value to the customer)
> In the *right way* (through standard work)
> With *continuous monitoring* of processes (through visual management systems)
> And *structured coaching* for everyone (using the scientific method).

At this point, these practices are not just public and codified—they're now table stakes for competing.

CONTINUOUS IMPROVEMENT

Competition is most often the proximate driver of improvement. If you personally don't get better, you won't make the team, or you won't get chosen for the orchestra. If a company (or industry) doesn't improve, it will go out of business. But the ultimate driver is an ethos of what the Japanese call *kaizen*, or "continuous improvement." This ethos dictates that there is always—always!—room for improvement. An individual can always be faster, stronger, more agile, more injury resistant, and have greater cardiovascular fitness. As pro football Hall of Famer Steve Young said,

> The principle is competing against yourself. It's about self-improvement, about being better than you were the day before.

In a business setting, products can always be less expensive, more reliable, easier to use, or more attractive. Processes can always be faster, simpler, or deliver higher-quality outputs. A continuous improvement mindset views quality and performance not as something fixed and immutable but as something worthy of endless labor. Carolyn Brodsky, the president of Sterling Rope, maintains, "There isn't a process that can't be improved, because customers always change, and you have to change with them." Fit companies embrace continuous improvement in all aspects of their operations, seeing excellence as a journey without a finish line.

Embracing continuous improvement means that there are really two parts to every job. The first part is the obvious one: actually doing the work listed in the job description. The second part of the job is what separates fit companies from the pretenders: the responsibility to improve the way the work is done. This aspect of the job is seldom formalized (have you ever seen a job description that included this responsibility?), yet it's an integral part of organizational fitness. After all, the larger organizational processes are composed of the individual processes contained within each job. You can't improve the whole without working on the parts.

Improving the work—making it easier, faster, less prone to defects—must be the responsibility of the person doing the job. Who else could be responsible for it? No one understands the intricacies of a job better than the person actually doing it, and therefore no one is better suited to design and implement those improvements. Outsourcing responsibility for this improvement to a team of Six Sigma Black Belts or external consultants, or foisting it onto the leadership team, is not only disrespectful to the true experts (the people doing the jobs), but it's not scalable, and it is unlikely to result in as much improvement.

Fit leaders understand that the responsibility—and authority—for job improvement lies with the people doing the work, and that insight fundamentally changes their approach to leadership. FastCap, a company that designs and manufactures woodworking tools, takes this idea so seriously that everyone's job title is "process engineer." Paul Akers, the CEO, tells a story about how he and a team of four senior engineers tried to improve a packaging step on an assembly line. The solution they came up with wasn't nearly as good as the one developed by the three people already working on the line:

> Between Heather, Annie, and Skyler, a 19-year-old kid, they came up with better ideas and more thoughtful solutions than myself (the lean expert), and four of my engineers. . . . They're smarter than I am. And the problem is, when we get to the top levels of leadership like myself, we start to think we're the smartest people in the group—and we're not. The people you're working with are so brilliant, it's unbelievable. But we're too stupid as leaders to find out, because we don't spend any time in their world.[5]

DRIVING OUT FEAR

In his book *Out of the Crisis*, the late W. Edwards Deming offered 14 key principles for management to follow that would significantly improve the effectiveness of any organization. Point number eight is "drive out fear." In his somewhat gnomic way of expressing himself (Deming seems never to have met a complex sentence or a dependent clause that he liked), he explained,

> We must break down the class distinctions between types of workers within the organization. . . . . Cease to blame employees for problems of the system. People need to feel secure to make suggestions. Management must follow through on suggestions. People on the job cannot work effectively if they dare not enquire into the purpose of the work that they do, and dare not offer suggestions for simplification and improvement of the system.[6]

"Fear" is a strong word—so strong that I'd bet most leaders don't think that fear runs through their organization. But careful reflection reveals anxiety—and yes, fear—that all the foosball tables, free massages, and Red Bull–stocked refrigerators can't eliminate. Employees are afraid that new methods or technology will make their skills obsolete and threaten their jobs. They're afraid that mistakes will be thrown in their face during the year-end performance evaluation. They're afraid of having management criticize, ridicule, or ignore their suggestions. They're afraid of being attacked for errors and failures, even if they're committed in the service of improvement. They're afraid of what's known in the healthcare field as "name, blame, and shame." Charles Kettering, the head of research at General Motors in the early twentieth century, famously said,

> The biggest job we have is to teach a newly hired employee how to fail intelligently. We have to train him to experiment over and over and to keep on trying and failing until he learns what will work.[7]

But what Kettering didn't state explicitly is that fit leaders must also teach employees how to experiment *properly* so that failures are educational and beneficial. They have to teach employees the scientific method in the form of the "Plan-Do-Study-Adjust" (PDSA) cycle that underlies continuous improvement.[8] But before they can teach this, fit leaders have to drive the fear out of the organization so that employees are willing to experiment in the first place.

The first, and perhaps most important, step to driving out fear is a fundamental shift in attitude toward problems. Most leaders hate problems. They want their operations and their processes to run smoothly. They get frustrated when something goes wrong. They blame people. They try to find out who is responsible for the problem. By contrast— and at the risk of sounding hyperbolic—fit leaders (and fit companies) love their problems. Problems are not things to be hidden. They're not things to fear. They're not even negative things—they're improvement opportunities in disguise. A fit leader frames a problem as nothing more threatening than the gap between where the organization is today and where it wants to be tomorrow. To that end, a fit leader tries to find out *why* the problem occurred, not *who* screwed up. (In fact, if someone did screw up, a fit leader asks why the system made it so easy for the person to screw up. The blame, such as it exists, is on the system, not the person. Why, not who.) When fit leaders do blame people for a problem, they point the finger at themselves. Larry Barrett, VP of operations at Sage Rods, views most problems as a signal that the leaders have erred. He explains:

> One thing that we do now in our team meetings is to publicly recognize the responsibility that the leaders have. Especially when we are talking about an obstacle or an area where we're not hitting our goals, I'll make a point of calling out my responsibility. I encourage my other leaders to emulate this type of accountability and transparency. A common example is when we're asking the team to work overtime. It's hard to think of a scenario where this is not my fault as the leader, and I make sure that the team knows (1) that I own this; (2) what I plan to do to fix it; and (3) how long it might take. We get better results with this style of communication.

The U.S. Navy's famous flight demonstration squad, the Blue Angels, epitomizes what it means to embrace problems as opportunities for improvement. Within an hour of their performance (which lasts about an hour), the pilots debrief for two to six hours. No visitors are allowed in the debrief sessions; the privacy and confidentiality of the review is necessary to create a safe environment for brutally honest feedback. Each pilot provides an assessment of his own performance and acknowledges errors or things he could have done better. As a group, they also review a videotape of the demonstration, frame by frame, to identify the root cause for any maneuver that's not perfect. You can imagine how fear-inducing these conversations could be— after all, a small mistake could easily result in a colleague's death. But it's this willingness to embrace problems, to look for why, not who, that has made them so successful.[9]

Reflection

Debrief. After-action review. Lessons learned. Reflection. These are some of the terms used by organizations to describe the formal or informal meeting held after projects conclude to examine how things went and what they can do better. Whatever word you use, a formalized, structured approach is essential to improvement.

It's tempting to use the debrief meeting as an opportunity to celebrate the successes, of course. After all, people have worked long and hard to complete the project or launch the new product. However, the real learning comes from an analysis of the errors or problems that came up over the course of the project. It's only by examining those problems that the organization can identify root causes and institute countermeasures for the next cycle. The Blue Angels' approach is a model of how to do it right. They reflect on every aspect of their performance in the same way, each time. (This ties into the notion of standard work that we'll discuss in Chapter 4.) They're afraid neither to acknowledge their own mistakes nor to point out the mistakes of others—sparing one's feelings is far less important than ensuring that everyone comes out alive.

Even if there were no obvious problems (which is highly unlikely), even if a project was completed flawlessly, the reflection period provides the opportunity to improve. Indeed, it's obligatory for a fit organization to provide opportunities to improve, because there is *always* room for improvement.

The fit organization has a mindset similar to that of an athlete who is always driven to be better at his sport. Problems—performance gaps—are there to be overcome, not hidden. As clichéd as it may be to hold up basketball great Michael Jordan as an exemplar, the truth is that he embodied this attitude. When he entered the NBA in 1984, critics said Jordan was just a guy who could slash his way to the basket and dunk—so he focused on developing his jump shot and became one of the premier shooters in the game. When critics accused him of being a one-dimensional offensive player, he focused on defense, leading the league in steals and turning himself into the Defensive Player of the Year. As he got older and lost his explosiveness, he transformed himself into one of the best post-up players in the NBA, with a nearly unstoppable fadeaway jump shot.[10] Even if you don't know anything about basketball, you can appreciate his constant drive for improvement, for relentlessly closing the gap between his current performance and where he wanted to be in the future. Jordan may be notorious for holding grudges and being thin-skinned about criticism, but he used the slings and arrows from his critics as motivation for improvement.

Just as an athlete knows that there is always room for improvement in fitness and skill level, fit companies know that there are always problems (gaps between the current state and the ideal condition) to be solved. If there don't seem to be any problems—well, that's a serious problem. Taiichi Ohno, pioneer of the Toyota Production System in the 1950s, said, "Having no problems is the biggest problem of all."[11] Thirty years later, Susumu Uchikawa, a general manager at the New United Motor Manufacturing Inc. (NUMMI) joint venture auto plant, went one step further: "No problem is problem! Managers' *job* is to see problems!"[12] Uchikawa's exhortation gets at the fundamental truth that there are always problems in any organization. It's only fear that keeps them hidden. The standard work that brings leaders to the front lines where work is being done (Chapter 4), combined with visual management systems (Chapter 5), helps an organization bring these problems to light and become fitter.

SMALL STEPS: THE RIGHT WAY TO IMPROVE

Instilling and nurturing a continuous improvement culture sets the fit organization up for long-term success. Conversely, adopting a change management strategy—looking to episodic, large-scale changes for dramatic improvement—is more likely to end in disappointment and frustration. It's the same as physical fitness. You don't go into the gym trying to deadlift 300 pounds on the first day, or try to run a 20-miler in your first workout. You build your way up to those levels. Similarly, you have to develop the organizational muscles required for continuous improvement through small steps. Trying to improve productivity in a process by 25 percent on the first try is a recipe for failure and frustration.

The data on change management are consistent: about 70 percent of change initiatives fail, despite the plethora of books, conferences, and scholarly papers dedicated to the subject.[13] The roots of those failures are varied and deep, but I believe that one of the issues is the attempt to do too much too soon—the organizational equivalent of going out for a 20-mile run on the first day of training. Organizations underestimate the difficulty and expense of designing, structuring, and implementing change. Particularly in today's more global business environment, with diverse teams working in different countries (to say nothing of different cultures), making and sustaining change is an order of magnitude more challenging than it was when even large enterprises were primarily located in one country.

Another powerful factor working against successful change is the short-circuiting of higher-level cognitive thinking that people experience when faced with major change. Dr. Robert Maurer, a professor of behavioral science at UCLA, explains that no matter how well intentioned the change, it triggers the fight-or-flight response seated in the amygdala, the "prehistoric" part of the brain. In working with patients, he's found that it's easier to get them to change unhealthy parts of their lifestyle through small, incremental modifications than through wholesale changes. For example, he had one patient begin an exercise program by simply marching in place for one minute in front of the television . . . then two minutes, then three, and so on. Having her sign up for a six-month CrossFit class would have triggered the fight-or-flight response, but one minute of marching in front of the TV? It's a small enough change that the amygdala didn't take over from the frontal lobe. The same dynamic occurs in the workplace: small changes or improvements circumvent the amygdala, making it easier for people to adopt and accept a new way of working. Take Fast-Cap: each employee's goal is to figure out how to do his or her job two seconds faster. Every day.

The continuous improvement approach to work dovetails with the research presented by Dan Pink in his book *Drive*. Pink argues that there are three essential components of human motivation: autonomy, mastery, and purpose. Carrots and sticks—rewards and punishments—are counterproductive in today's knowledge-intensive work environments. Instead, people need to have a degree of independence in determining what work they do and how they do it (autonomy); they need to feel that they're developing skills and improving (mastery); and they need to feel a connection to something larger than themselves (purpose). A commitment to improvement feeds those first two needs. Workers have the freedom to select both the problems that they're going to tackle and the methods by which they're going to try to fix them, and they gain a sense of mastery as they improve their problem-solving skills.

You can see this dynamic at Quality Bicycle Products (QBP), a distributor of bicycle parts and accessories. QBP's "Great Results Improving Processes" (GRIP) program generates hundreds of improvement ideas each year. Fifty percent of the company's annual cost savings come from the "little GRIP" program, smaller ideas that can be implemented relatively easily, without additional investment in equipment or technology. For example, the workers in the distribution center identified a way to eliminate extra walking distance in picking and packing products for shipment. The savings was small for each individual basket of products: only about 10 seconds per basket. But the savings to the company over the course of the year was nearly $60,000 in labor hours. This improvement hit all three points raised by Dan Pink: autonomy (the workers identified and selected the problem to work on); mastery (they came up with a better process); and purpose (they could ship more boxes each day, getting products to waiting customers faster).

The commitment to improvement also ties into the findings of Harvard professor Teresa Amabile. In her book *The Progress Principle*, Amabile suggests that the simple act of making progress in one's work causes people to enjoy their work more and be more intrinsically motivated. This finding may not strike you as a Copernican insight, but when you consider how often employees are asked to simply come to the office or factory and do the same job, the same way, every day (think fryer station at McDonald's, or window teller in a bank), you can begin to understand why engagement levels are so low and turn-over is so high in many organizations. Amabile says,

> The most important implication of the progress principle is this: By support-ing people and their daily progress in meaningful work, managers improve not only the inner work lives of their employees but also the organization's long-term performance, which enhances inner work life even more.[14]

An organization that truly commits to continuous improvement pro-vides the opportunity for its people to make daily progress, with all the benefits that entails. Sterling Rope, a U.S.-based manufacturers of rope for climbing, rescue, arbor, military, industrial, and work uses, has reaped those benefits in a variety of ways. Among other improvements at Ster-ling, employees in production, R&D, and marketing came up with bet-ter ways of managing work-in-process inventory, as well as improving the packaging, labeling, and storing of finished-goods inventory. They even redesigned the packaging to incorporate three different hangtags and two labels and changed how they closed the bag. These changes doubled the volume of ropes pushed through the final finish area without increasing headcount—part of the reason the company's profit margin is more than double the average for manufacturers of its size. More significantly, the constant and expected involvement in improvement work has led to a remarkable level of employee engagement and retention (many workers have been there for 15 out of the company's 20 years, and most people have been there for at least 10 years), and the company is inundated with job applicants when it has an open position.

Continuous Improvement . . . of People

Now that I've spent the better part of this chapter arguing that a con-tinuous improvement philosophy is vital to making processes work better, let me shift gears and suggest that this isn't the real benefit of continuous improvement at all. Sure, your processes will be better, faster, and produce higher-quality outputs—and all of that is important. But even more valuable is the growth and development of your people. Creating and nurturing an atmosphere of continuous improvement ensures that your employees will develop the skills needed for success (their own and your organization's) in a volatile, unpredictable world. Author and consultant Michael Ballé goes so far as to argue that companies should start their problem-solving and improvement efforts with small, relatively trivial problems before tackling bigger issues. The goal is to use problem solving as a teaching device, similar to the way doctors are trained by problem-based teaching.[15] From this perspective, you can (and should) start your continuous improvement activities by figuring out a way to keep the coffee pot from running out before you start worrying about 100-percent on-time deliveries. In fact, Hydro Flask, an Oregon-based maker of insulated metal containers for personal use, began its continuous improvement journey with precisely this problem: how to keep the coffee pot from running out (which is not a trivial issue in Oregon.) That small step has led Hydro Flask to identify improvements in manufacturing, recycling, and better ways of embedding its core values in employees' daily work. In other words, people development, not fixing the process in its entirety, is the ultimate—and highest—goal of a continuous improvement culture.

It may sound a bit odd, but a company that commits to continuous improvement creates an organization filled with scientists—or at least, scientific thinkers. All workers, from shipping clerks to product engineers, from accounts payable staff to inventory planners, become proficient in the scientific method of problem solving: understanding a problem; formulating a hypothesis about why that problem exists; developing an experiment or countermeasure to test that hypothesis; and finally, evaluating the result to see whether the hypothesis was proved or disproved.

FIGURE 1.1 The Shewhart cycle.

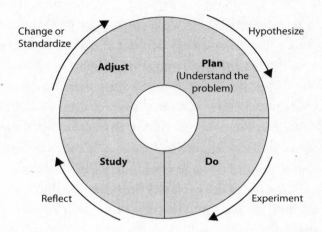

Outside of eighth-grade science class, this process is usually called the Deming or Shewhart Cycle (see Figure 1.1), and it is typically expressed as PDSA: Plan-Do-Study-Adjust. If you want a more interesting and compelling illustration of PDSA thinking, tune into TV's *Mythbusters*. Although the *Mythbusters* team has a great time blowing up a lot of stuff, it's all carefully planned and done in the context of structured scientific thinking.

It's hard to overstate the value of rigorous scientific thinking. On a global level, we'd still be living in caves wearing animal pelts, hunting wildebeest, and gathering goji berries if it weren't for some scientific thinkers who figured out that if they planted seeds at the right time, they could harvest wheat a few months later. We'd also still think everything was made of earth, air, fire, and water, that "bad air" caused disease, and that the sun revolved around the earth. But even on the more prosaic level of your day job, scientific thinking is nearly as important. Its emphasis on making improvements based on close analysis of the work itself, rather than internal politics, personal agendas, or wishful thinking, aligns people around common goals and fosters productive dialogue around problems. PDSA sets the stage for true learning and improvement.

Sadly, most organizations don't engage in Plan-Do-Study-Adjust. They rush to the Do phase and typically stall out there. (Presumably that would be noted as DDDD.) If you've ever had your VP of sales replaced or hired a new ad agency because sales were down, or suffered through a reorganization for any reason at all, you know what I'm talking about. These moves tend to be knee-jerk reactions to problems that aren't fully understood, and the efficacy of these changes is seldom assessed, either because the organization has no metrics for evaluation or because it lacks the discipline to do so. Once the new business cards are printed and people's desks have moved, it's business as usual. Or at least it is until the next sales hiccup. With scientific thinking, however, we don't act until we have a solid grasp of the root cause of the problem, and that reduces the likelihood that we'll waste time, money, and effort trying to improve the situation.

Developing this thinking process is essential for long-term success, whether you're an athlete or a coach, a CEO or a frontline worker. Along with death and taxes, change is the only certainty in life, and an organization that doesn't have the ability to engage in rigorous PDSA thinking will not have the ability to adapt to those changes.

It's worth mentioning that embracing scientific thinking addresses one of Teresa Amabile's key findings—that setbacks generate fear and reduce motivation. This insight isn't really breaking news. But a PDSA approach eliminates the fear, because there are no real setbacks—only experiments that, regardless of how they turn out, still get you one step closer to a solution. As Adam Savage, host of *Mythbusters*, said, "There is really no such thing as a failed experiment. Any test that yields valid data is a valid test." That's not to say that people won't get frustrated, irritated, angry, and demoralized when they're unable to solve a problem or make an improvement. I'm pretty sure that Thomas Edison had more than a few expletive-filled temper tantrums en route to nailing the light bulb. (He may have been a genius, but he was still human.)

But as he famously said about his numerous unsuccessful attempts to find the right material for a light bulb filament, "I haven't failed. I've just found 10,000 ways that won't work."

CREATING THE CULTURE

Organizations don't naturally turn toward continuous improvement. It takes focused, concerted effort on the part of leadership to create that kind of behavior and that kind of culture. I won't go into too much detail on this point—the library is filled with books on culture change—but I will mention some key points to consider, which I've adapted from author's excellent work on this topic:[16]

> *State your commitment to continuous improvement—and explain why.* In most organizations there's a real "flavor of the month" problem with new initiatives, often because the underlying rationale hasn't been articulated. HR initiatives in particular are received with this sort of cynicism, and you can understand why: most people don't see how self-identifying as a Myers-Briggs ENTJ is going to affect the quality of the new product development process—or their bonus at the end of the year. Fit leaders live the gospel of continuous improvement and continually show how it directly improves the organization by connecting it to the larger goals and strategy.
>
> *Participate, don't proclaim.* Nothing is more toxic to the establishment of a continuous improvement culture than hypocrisy. A fit leader participates in improvement activities herself. It doesn't matter whether those are projects that she's leading or projects that she's just involved with—the key element is regular participation. People need to see that you

value improvement enough to invest your own time and energy into the same activities you're asking them to commit to.

Challenge people for improvement—and challenge again. Organizational inertia is a powerful thing. You're not going to overcome it and shift the prevailing culture by asking people to do one project. Or two. Or five. People are busy with their daily responsibilities, and it's natural for them to get caught up in doing their jobs. As a leader, you need to continually challenge them to find more improvements. James Cotter, VP of manufacturing at the outdoor products company Cascade Designs, says, "It's nearly impossible to permanently embed a continuous improvement mindset in the culture. As soon as senior leadership stops asking for improvement, you plateau or slip back." This kind of ongoing pursuit of improvement can be emotionally difficult—people may feel that they can never satisfy you. ("Jeez, will you leave me alone for just a *little* while?") But this challenge is actually a sign of respect: respect for people's existing skills and their capacity for growth and learning. Pushing people to grow and improve doesn't necessarily make you an unreasonable slave driver, as long as you support them in their pursuit of improvement.

Give people time to improve. If you're going to ask people to devote time to improving the organization's operations, you need to give them time to do it. And make no mistake about it: committing to improvement through structured PDSA thinking means regularly devoting time and attention to it. Fit organizations consciously design each step of a process, study the results, and then engage in another round of redesign. This cycle is a time-consuming process. Google and 3M garner a lot of press for their "20 percent time"—free time for people to work on new products and projects. I'll suggest that if creating something new is worth 20 percent, surely improving every facet of the way the company operates is worth at least 6 percent (30 minutes a day). In fact, at Quality Bike Parts, managers are responsible for helping employees get time to implement their improvement ideas by redistributing work, bringing in temp labor, shifting schedules, and so on.

Make ideas visible, and respond to them—quickly. Mark Graban points out that a Google search for "suggestion box" leads to page after page of boxes with padlocks. I'm not entirely sure where the notion came from that employee suggestions should be kept under lock and key like dangerous animals, but the classic suggestion box is where good ideas go to die. Suggestion boxes also don't do much to encourage suggestions: the Philadelphia VA regional office recently received a grand total of two suggestions (one asked for "very stylish" golf shirts; the other critiqued the box itself) in the first month that it was installed. Instead, post improvement ideas in public so that everyone can see them—and then respond quickly, within a few days. Quality Bike Parts' policy is that managers must respond to "little GRIP" ideas within 48 hours, and those that are selected must be implemented within three weeks. Fit companies know that if you don't respond to all comments, you increase the likelihood that people will see your actions as faux empowerment: a cosmetic, HR-driven program and not a genuine effort to engage employees in a process of continuous improvement.

Focus on increasing customer value, not on cost savings. As I explain in Chapter 2, cutting expenses is not particularly inspiring. People are energized when they can make improvements that create more value, provide better customer service, and make their colleagues' lives (and their own) easier. Asking people to find cost savings is emotionally and spiritually desiccating, and it is a guaranteed dead end.

Expect (some) failure. If you're running experiments, you'll inevitably fail to make improvements some of the time. That's the nature of the scientific method. Don't criticize people for not succeeding. The Silicon Valley mantra these days is "fail fast." That's not carte blanche for failure all the time, but it should be license to experiment without fear of failure. Remember that perhaps the most important outcome of continuous improvement is a more skilled, insightful, and capable workforce.

Listen carefully for complaints. Sometimes it's hard for people to think of an improvement they can make. By contrast, it's usually pretty easy for them to find things to complain about. Fortunately, every complaint is a nascent improvement opportunity. Seize upon those complaints and challenge people to solve them. Carolyn Brodsky of Sterling Rope says, "Pay attention to the moment when someone says, 'Are we still having that problem?' or, 'I thought we fixed that!' That's a good place to look for improvement opportunities."

Don't crowd out intrinsic rewards. There's ample research showing that extrinsic rewards such as money crowd out intrinsic rewards. If you provide large cash bonuses or other significant benefits for successfully completing an improvement project, you'll likely destroy the intrinsic rewards of the project: the pride that people take in doing a good job, solving tough problems, and accomplishing something meaningful to their colleagues and their customers. James Cotter at Cascade Designs gives people who complete their first project a "kaizen T-shirt" and says that people wear them with pride.

Recognize and celebrate. Closely related to the idea of intrinsic rewards is the human desire for recognition. When someone successfully introduces an improvement, make it public, and do it when the improvement is made. Don't wait for a monthly or quarterly all-hands meeting. Ring a bell, make an announcement, do an interpretive dance, whatever suits your organizational culture. Celebrate a job well done, and give people the incalculable reward of recognition among their peers.

Drive out fear. I made this point earlier, but it's so important that it bears repeating. Your team won't embrace improvement if people are afraid that their ideas will be dismissed, disparaged, or ignored by their bosses. They won't embrace improvement if they're afraid they'll be labeled a whiner. And they most certainly won't embrace improvement if they're afraid that their improvements will cost them (or their coworkers) their jobs. You must make it absolutely clear that no one will lose his or her employment as a result of an improvement. Some may lose their position—that is, they may need to be moved to a new department if their role is no longer necessary—but they will still have a home in the organization.

The pursuit of organizational fitness is like the pursuit of physical fitness. There are no secret formulas, no magic potions, no shortcuts to the promised land. Both kinds of fitness require continual focus and commitment to the hard work of improvement. When you accept your current physical or organizational limitations and weaknesses as opportunities for growth and see the never-ending journey toward perfection as something inherently worthwhile, you've taken the first step to driving out fear and unleashing the power of your employees.

Monday Morning To-Do List

Here are some important first steps to begin embedding a commitment to fitness in your organization.

- Design a suggestion form. At the very least, you'll want to capture whose idea it is, what problem the person is trying to solve, the date suggested and the date implemented, and a space for managerial approval. Start with the basics, and over time you can modify it to identify PDSA phases, photographs, and more. It doesn't have to be perfect from the start. It has to be simple to fill out and visible.
- Create a space for suggestion forms in each work area. Consider creating a "hall of fame" in a central location for particularly dramatic or well-executed improvements.
- Determine what rewards (if any) you'll provide to people who submit and complete improvements. Remember that rewards should be small—movie tickets, discount cards to retailers, free car wash coupons, and so on—so as not to crowd out the intrinsic motivation for improvement. You could even create a point system—one point for making a suggestion and one point when it's implemented—and then allow employees to "spend" these points on products in a gift catalog.
- Schedule an all-hands meeting to explain what you're doing and why. Don't expect people to immediately rally to the cause, however. It will require repetition and storytelling to convince people that you're serious.
- Provide people time to work on improvements. Arrange hourly workers' schedules so that they have some time each day (or at the very least, each week) to step away from their daily work. For salaried workers who aren't driven by the time clock, consider joining them for some of their improvement projects. Create visual trackers to show how much time, and how often, each person is working on a project.

2

Increase Value, Don't Cut Costs

*L*eaders err when they use cost cutting to reach financial targets. Long-term success requires that leaders focus on increasing the value that their organizations deliver to customers. Managing exclusively by financial results is ineffective in creating real value, since it leads only to transient benefits. Financial numbers are by definition lagging indicators, so by the time leadership takes action, it's already too late. The damage to the organization's reputation and customer satisfaction has already been done. By contrast, fit companies manage by means. They monitor, fix, and improve their operational processes in real time. Figuring out how to increase the value created by any process yields both happier customers and, inevitably, lower costs.*

Don't go on a diet. Don't try to lose weight. And if you're a business, don't try to cut costs.

Do improve your time to market. Do lower your defect rate. Do build the flexibility to serve different customers in different ways. Do strive for zero accidents.

Real fitness isn't defined by overall weight or by body fat percentage. Sure, if you're 5´6″ and weigh as much as a double-door Sub-Zero refrigerator, you should probably put down the box of Twinkies. But if you're a 5´10″ fashion runway model tipping the scales at 102 pounds soaking wet, you're probably not very fit either. Skinny, yes. Employable in Paris and Milan, definitely. But not especially fit. Real fitness isn't just about body mass index. It includes cardiovascular capacity, muscular strength, and flexibility. And if you're an athlete—even a recreational one—you also need coordination, agility, speed, and quickness. You can't gain those capabilities just by dieting.

To be sure, improving fitness requires healthy eating (and maybe even a little dieting). Mo Farah, the British distance runner who won gold medals in the 5,000-meter and 10,000-meter races in both the 2012 Olympics and the 2013 World Championships, eats pasta, steamed vegetables, and grilled chicken. For both lunch and dinner. Every day. (Although he did celebrate his Olympic triumph by allowing himself a single hamburger after the final race. Consider it the four-year burger.) But true fitness goes far beyond that. It requires exercises to build strength and flexibility, speed and stamina, aerobic capacity, and injury resistance. Weight loss—or in the case of these elite athletes, weight maintenance—comes as a result of their exercise and their fitness regimens. Weight loss is an ancillary benefit, not the goal of their efforts.

There's an organizational parallel here: a company can't get fit simply by cutting costs. To be sure, it can improve its income statement in the short term by laying off workers, closing offices, banning color copies, and getting rid of the coffee machine. That's not going to make the organization fit, however, because organizational fitness isn't just about low expenses. It includes the ability to react quickly to market shifts, to create and deliver new products and services, and to continually improve process efficiency and effectiveness—all in the service of delivering greater value to customers. Cutting expenses as a way to organizational fitness is like cutting calories as a way to personal fitness. At its logical extreme, it results in corporate anorexia nervosa—a feeble organization filled with dispirited employees unable to compete in the marketplace and serve customers. Sunbeam Corporation is the poster child for this misguided approach. Sunbeam hired "Chainsaw Al" Dunlap in 1996 to turn the company around. Within a year, he had laid off half the company's staff (6,000 people) and eliminated 90 percent of the company's products. Some said that he had gone too far, cutting muscle and not just fat.[1] They were right: by 2001, the company was bankrupt.

There's another parallel between dieting and simple expense cutting: neither works in the long term. It's common knowledge that the vast majority of people who lose weight on a diet regain it within a year or so. That may be partly due to a lack of discipline or a failure of willpower. But there's more to it than that. When obese people embark on a weight-loss program, the body actually fights to regain the weight it has lost. It acts as though it's in danger of starvation (even if the person is still overweight) and pulls out all the metabolic stops to encourage more food consumption. It produces more ghrelin, a gastric hormone that stimulates hunger, and generates less peptide YY and leptin, hormones that suppress hunger.[2]

Organizations that simply cut expenses tend not to maintain their new weight either—they also fight to regain the weight that's been shed. More often than not, there's no concomitant reduction in work—it simply gets shifted around after layoffs. Employees take on the additional responsibilities of a colleague or a boss. They work longer and harder, but because the underlying processes aren't functioning any better, and because these companies haven't focused on improving *how* they operate, work doesn't get done faster, better, or more easily. Eventually, after the financial crisis passes, the organization brings back the coffee machine, permits color copies, and caters meetings again. Travel restrictions are lifted. Gradually, the company hires people to refill the roles that were eliminated earlier. The weight comes back on, and the organization is just a market downturn away from another round of layoffs and cost cutting. McKinsey & Company detailed this situation in late 2009, as the economic recovery following the Great Recession began to pick up steam:

> An international energy company that needed to save money fast started by simply defining the amount of savings it needed and then required each department to cut costs by a similar amount, primarily through head count reductions, which varied from 17 to 22 percent. The reality, however, was that the company needed to invest more in certain technological areas that were changing quickly, as well as in operations, where performance was far below industry benchmarks. What's more, the HR and IT departments substantially duplicated certain activities because different layers in the organization were doing similar things. Much deeper cuts could therefore be made in these functions, with little strategic risk. But the company cut costs across the board, and just six months later, technology and operations were lobbying hard to bring in new staff to take on an "uncontrollable workload," while substantial duplication remained in HR and IT.[3]

The truth is that most companies treat expense reduction as a one-time exercise. When the pressure is off, expenses come back, because the company hasn't invested in building internal capabilities and improving processes. Nearly half of the executives in a recent survey by the consultancy Strategy& acknowledged that their companies cut costs due to external events or outside pressure, not due to a culture of continuous improvement.[4] In fact, some research shows that only 10 percent of cost reduction programs show sustained results three years later.[5] Like a person whose health efforts concentrate on weight loss through fad diets, the fat comes back. Always.

The alternative is for organizations to focus on building fitness, not on reducing costs. In this context, fitness means becoming faster, more agile, and better able to take advantage of new opportunities and serve customers better. It means examining the processes by which the organization operates. It means focusing on the means by which work is done, not the (financial) ends. A corporate "fitness program" develops employees' capacity to solve problems and improve performance, with the long-term goal of increasing the value provided to customers. And with greater customer value comes improved financial performance. In fact, cost reduction is an inevitable outcome of the pursuit of fitness—but cost reduction is not the primary objective. If it were, the organization could simply lay off workers and beat up suppliers for better prices, which, as we've seen, yields only short-term benefits.

There's another problem when organizations focus on cost reduction: it's a demoralizing, zero-sum exercise. It's dispiriting for everyone involved with the organization, generating fear and anxiety for all people involved. By contrast, increasing fitness is energizing and exciting, because there are so many ways to do it, and there's always more that can be done. Author Mark Graban tells this story about a workshop he led at a hospital:

> The nurse manager told me, "I thought we were supposed to come up with ideas for reducing costs. I couldn't think of any. But, when you explained that kaizen [continuous improvement] was about saving time, making our work easier, and improving patient care, I realized I had a lot of ideas after all!"
>
> In my experience, healthcare professionals generally don't get excited about the department's budget or the hospital's bottom line. They just don't think about those things very much. They're thinking about their patients, and they're annoyed by problems and waste that get in the way of providing the best care to them.[6]

Management by Means vs. Management by Results

Most leaders manage by results. They examine the monthly and quarterly financial reports and make operational decisions based on that information. Unfortunately, those numbers are lagging indicators—by the time an issue manifests itself in those reports, the problems have been persisting for several months. Even if you reduced the financial reporting time frame to one week or one day, those numbers still only show what happened in the past. When you think about it, making decisions about organizational priorities and performance based on trailing financial data is like trying to drive by looking in the rearview mirror.

In his book *Profit Beyond Measure*, Tom Johnson introduced a better alternative to this approach—what he called "management by means." Management by means entails close and direct observation of how the myriad processes that run through any organization are operating. (The standard work described in Chapter 4 and the visual management systems described in Chapter 5 make this observation possible.) Rather than waiting to see the downstream financial consequences of a problem in a process, you can see it crop up in real time and can institute countermeasures *before* it has a financial impact.

To take a simple example, distribution center workers at Quality Bicycle Products (QBP), a distributor of bike parts and accessories, were having difficulty keeping up with demand. The company didn't wait for the month-end numbers to see that problem. VP Jerry Pomije noticed that the workers were missing necessary shipping supplies—they didn't have enough boxes, box cutters, or tape guns to pack and ship smoothly and quickly—so he helped create a system to solve this problem.

The power of close observation is so great that Larry Barrett, VP of operations at Sage, a manufacturer of fly rods and fishing reels, gave away his office and moved his desk to the production floor. He wanted the ability to see problems first-hand and deal with them immediately. As he says, "It's all about the process. We [American companies] are way too goal focused. Achieving the goal is an outcome of getting the process right."

Sometimes it's easy to increase fitness by improving the process. In the case of QBP above, direct observation of how the work is being done revealed the problem quickly. But the issues aren't always as clear as the lack of tape guns and box cutters. To make more subtle problems visible, you need to create metrics and targets that tell you how the process is running. Many of the metrics will relate to the customer (either the ultimate customer, or just the next step in the process). Some of them—like quality—won't tie directly to the customer but obviously affect the ultimate performance of the system.

For example, in 2006, at Franciscan St. Francis Health in Indianapolis, the emergency room (ER) was performing so poorly that it ranked in the 13th percentile in patient satisfaction, meaning 87 percent of hospitals were performing better than it in patient satisfaction. Although it was recently named a top 100 hospital in the country for overall quality by Healthgrades (which put it in the top 2 percent of all hospitals for quality patient care), it wasn't satisfying its customers' expectation for fast service. Joe Swartz, the director of continuous improvement, led a team to improve this number by focusing on two of the key drivers of satisfaction: the time it took from arrival at the ER till the patient saw the doctor (door to provider), and the time from arrival to departure (door to discharge).

Although it sounds simple, this wasn't an easy shift to make: the nurses and physicians weren't accustomed to it, and they worried that it would encourage shortcutting of the process and lead to a reduction in the quality of patient care.

Swartz allayed those fears by explaining that irrespective of any changes they made, the quality of care was nonnegotiable—they had to provide either the same or a higher level of care. However, the process could be simplified to reduce the delays, motion, travel, and frustrations that got in the way of providing that care. Then he showed them the data: in 2006, the average door-to-provider time was 45 minutes, which was the biggest factor in the low patient satisfaction scores. By engaging staff to solve the problems that made their jobs so difficult, they were able to make dramatic improvement. Table 2.1 shows some of the recent data:

TABLE 2.1   Franciscan St. Francis Health drivers of patient satisfaction

Measure	2011	After April 2012
Door to Provider (Median)	28 minutes	12 minutes
Door to Discharge (Median)	180 minutes	130 minutes
Left Without Treatment	2.8%	< 0.5%
Patient Satisfaction	13th percentile	> 50th percentile

This improvement didn't occur overnight. It took seven years of progressively more aggressive projects. The breakthrough was the realization that all the ER rooms filled up by midday, forcing new patients to wait for a long time before rooms opened up. (Of course, this wasn't apparent until the team focused on the impediments to providing care quickly.) Swartz's team decided it could increase the velocity at which patients moved through the rooms by radically redesigning the process. The new process moved lower-acuity patients from room to room (each room with a unique purpose) as they progressed through their stay, rather than occupying a single room for the duration. This change freed up individual ER rooms for new patients, creating additional room capacity.

This change increased patient satisfaction in several ways. First, it enabled patients who were in pain to be diagnosed and receive pain medication faster. Second, shorter door-to-provider time reduced patient anxieties. Third, moving patients from an Intake Room to a Procedure Room to the Lounge and finally to a Discharge area made them feel that they were waiting less.

Franciscan St. Francis Health has improved processes in other areas throughout the hospital as well. Over the past eight years, employees have identified and implemented over 23,000 improvements, saving millions of dollars. Of course, the hospital does track the results (patient satisfaction and percentage of patients leaving without treatment), but the critical measurement it watches now is the length of time patients are waiting. That's customer (patient) value.

It's worth noting that as an administrator, Swartz was deeply influenced by his earlier experience as a competitive wrestler. He was a state champion, won the Mideast Regional Olympic Wrestling Trials, placed ninth in the Olympic trials, and trained with the Olympic team in Colorado Springs. While training with the team, he noticed that the best wrestlers didn't focus very much on fancy wrestling moves. Rather, they spent most of their time practicing the basic techniques over and over again. This was revelatory. He saw that the key to excellence in both athletics and in business was to become extraordinarily good at the fundamentals—like getting patients through the ER faster.

In a similar fashion, Black Diamond Equipment, a maker of outdoor apparel and equipment, was struggling to meet customer demand for some of its product. The VP of manufacturing, Wim de Jager, realized that downtime of critical machines at the factory was a major factor affecting the company's ability to ship on time—but he couldn't see the downtime easily. He installed red lights that indicated when machines were down, and then he connected the whole system to a clock so he and his production team could measure the total downtime each week. This measurement made clear just how much time was being lost and galvanized the company's resolve to deal with the problem. Within three months the team was able to reduce downtime from 45 percent to 20 percent—allowing the company to meet customer demand and ship product on time.

Notice that neither of these organizations used poor results as an excuse to cut costs. Instead, they focused on fitness: managing by means to increase their ability to provide customer value by improving their processes—and that, inevitably, led to better results (see Table 2.2).

TABLE 2.2   Focus on value rather than cost-cutting

Traditional Organization: Focus on Cost Cutting	Fit Organization: Focus on Value
Manages "by the numbers" (period-end financial reports)	Manages by means—how the internal processes are running
Focuses on cost containment and cost reduction	Focuses on increasing value to customers
Sees gap between current and future states as justification for criticism	Sees gap between current and future states as opportunity for growth
Uses financial and cost accounting metrics to allocate costs to departments	Creates metrics to measure individual process speed, efficiency, quality, and safety
Poor results lead to layoffs, outsourcing, and a shift to part-time employees	Poor results lead to closer examination of processes
Coaching and development run through HR	All leaders and managers responsible for coaching and development
Episodic, event-based training	Continual training and coaching

GOAL SETTING—THE RIGHT WAY

I wasn't there, but I'm pretty confident that when Mo Farah (Olympic gold in the 5,000 and 10,000 meters, London 2012) began thinking about competing in the Olympics, he and his coach talked about more than just the need to run a specific time in each race. I also wasn't there when Roger Federer began his assault on the tennis record books, nor when Tiger Woods began his epic run of PGA majors wins, but I'm pretty sure that their plans were far more detailed than hitting more winners or shooting a lower score. All of these athletes set an ultimate goal (winning gold, winning Wimbledon, winning the Masters) and then worked with their coaches to build the specific skills necessary so that they could be in a position to win. Mo Farah needed to develop a final 400-meter kick to outrun the Kenyans and Ethiopians. Federer needed to be better at the net. Tiger needed to develop a short game. All great athletes break down their strengths and weaknesses and work to enhance the former and eliminate the latter. They focus on the means to the end, not simply the end itself.

Fit organizations take the same approach. They don't simply hold a two-day retreat where the executives set lofty goals without input from the managers and frontline employees who actually do the work. Instead, fit companies incorporate the front line into the planning exercise itself so as to connect the overarching goals with the necessary process-level improvements. After all, it's one thing to say that you want to improve patient satisfaction scores (the ultimate goal); it's quite another to work with your staff to figure out how to discharge patients more quickly (the means to the end).

As you consider where you want to take your organization, it's essential that you examine your key processes with your team to understand where the weaknesses are. What process obstacles block the way to delivering greater value? Or if there are no obstacles today, what processes will enable you to reach a higher level of performance and deliver greater value to the customer? How will you reduce the waiting time in the emergency department? How will you design and develop new products more quickly? How will you increase the number of outbound customer calls to proactively serve your retail customers rather than wait for them to call you? Table 2.3 provides some ideas of what these process-oriented metrics might look like.

TABLE 2.3   Process-oriented metrics

Function	Sample Process Metrics
HR	Number of times an interview was rescheduled Percent of new hires that have everything ready on their first day (computer passwords, keys, etc.)
Surgery (Healthcare)	Hospital-acquired infection rate OR utilization rate Number of times procedures were delayed/rescheduled due to incorrect patient prep
Product Development	Number of spec changes after finalization Percent of sales samples delivered on time Time from concept to first prototype
Customer Service	Customer satisfaction Time required to respond to inquiries Customer renewal rate
Manufacturing Line	Machine downtime Defect rate
Finance	Percent of A/R less than 90 days Time to cash

Of course, you'll want to work with your team to determine the relevant key performance indicators (KPIs) for your organization. These KPIs will focus your activities and efforts on the improvements that will enable you to attain your overarching goals.

CHILDREN'S MEDICAL CENTER: SERVING PATIENTS FASTER

With rapidly rising medical costs and lower reimbursements, hospitals in the United States are under enormous financial pressure. For the most part, they've dealt with this issue through traditional cost-reduction strategies: negotiating lower prices and more advantageous contracts with vendors, standardizing product choices, laying off staff, reducing contributions to retirement plans, and cutting or freezing salaries. Even if you don't closely follow the financial performance of companies in the healthcare industry, you probably know that this approach hasn't solved anything.

A major children's medical center in the United States faces the same financial challenges as any other hospital, but it has taken a different approach. Although cost containment is still important, it's no longer leadership's sole method of dealing with financial pressures. Instead, the hospital is building organizational capacity to increase the value it can provide to patients. The radiology department is a terrific example of how this shift in focus has paid off both for the hospital and for its patients.

This children's hospital is far and away the premier pediatric hospital in its community: if your kid is sick, you're taking him or her there. But in 2007, the hospital was losing patients needing MRIs to other facilities. Parents were going elsewhere because they had to wait 16 weeks for an MRI appointment. (It's actually more accurate to say "about 16 weeks"—according to one of the senior staff directors, when the hospital started analyzing its workflow and patient throughput, the directors realized they didn't even know what the actual wait times were.) Most people in the section thought that the wait was "only" 8 to 12 weeks, but that was only because the radiology department didn't have a robust system for tracking the requests that came in on scraps of paper, in faxes, or via phone calls. You can imagine that no matter how good the care was at this hospital, parents weren't going to wait four months to get an MRI. In fact, the situation had deteriorated to the point that the hospital's medical director demanded that one day per week on the schedule be reserved just for inpatient MRIs so that the other services in the hospital could take care of their patients. While understandable, that just made the wait times worse for outpatient scans.

As I mentioned earlier, organizational fitness means becoming faster and more agile, with the goal of serving customers better.

Realizing that the situation was untenable, and seeing that no cost-cutting program in the world would improve the situation, the radiology department set about reducing wait times. The staff members learned how to map patient flows and solve problems through root cause analyses. They identified bottlenecks in the system and created standardized templates to make the scheduling process consistent. Recognizing the power of making work visible, they developed a system to make incoming MRI requests visible to everyone. With no increase in the number of machines or staff, the hospital reduced wait times to two weeks or less and was even able to schedule next-day appointments for urgent cases. The focus on increasing the value provided to patients—faster access to MRI appointments—resulted in happier patients, less stressed employees, and smoother flow for the hospital's other departments. Better utilization of the machines also generated an additional $5 million in revenue for the department per year.

Like most healthcare organizations, this hospital still has plenty of problems that it needs to solve. An additional $5 million isn't a panacea for all of them. But it does mean that the hospital doesn't have to lay off people or cut salaries in the department. In fact, the radiology department's success shows that it's possible to provide better service and increase revenue without spending money. Even more important, though, is the increase in organizational fitness—solving the patient flow problem increased employees' capacity to improve processes and solve other problems.

Wild Things Gear: Having It Your Way

If you're an outdoor enthusiast, you know how exciting it is when you find a piece of clothing that fits your needs perfectly: it fits just right, it looks just right, and it has all the technical features that you need and want. Maybe you live in a rainy environment, and you want a waterproof jacket with a hood for hiking. Or perhaps you want a lighter, thinner, and softer fabric on the outside for your bike rides. Or maybe you just want something in orange. Unfortunately, it's not always so easy to find that perfect piece of apparel because your clothing options are, to a large extent, determined by decisions made 18 months earlier by a bunch of designers and developers you'll never meet, and who may very well not engage in the activities you love. Moreover, even if a company did make the *perfect* jacket for you, you might not see it unless you were lucky enough that your local retailer liked waterproof, hooded orange jackets with a zippered chest-pocket on the right side enough to bring them in and put them on the shelves.

Wild Things Gear makes technical apparel that consumers can customize for their own needs. CEO Ed Schmults believes that customization is especially important for technical clothing because it allows customers to create the functionality that's important to them, whether that's for ice climbing, skiing, or just tramping through the woods with the dog. Of course, customization is nice for fashion reasons as well. As Schmults says, "Who am I to tell a customer his jacket is ugly?"

Product customization is impossible if you manufacture in Asia (like virtually all outdoor companies). Asian factories are built for mass production: long production runs of hundreds or thousands of garments with minimal variation. It's also tough to get products to consumers quickly if they're produced halfway around the world—ocean shipping, customs clearance, and logistics (ocean port to warehouse to consumer) add three to four weeks of transit time. Airfreight is much faster, of course, but it's cost prohibitive for the company since most consumers aren't willing to pay for that service.

Schmults realized that to deliver the increased value that comes with a customized product, he'd have to develop the ability to make clothing in the United States. He'd have to get faster, more productive, and more skilled in apparel manufacturing—a tough job, given that the domestic apparel industry has been eviscerated over the past 20 years as companies have closed their factories and outsourced their work to Asia. However, using lean manufacturing techniques such as cellular production, one-piece flow, kitting of components, etc.— along with extensive training—Schmults was successful in making technical outdoor gear in the United States. Now, with a website that allows customers to configure their products online, domestic production, and the elimination of retailers for distribution, consumers can go from designing their own jacket to delivery at their house in only 14 days.

So, more value to the consumer—but what about the company? Moving away from traditional overseas mass production has meant faster production, less finished-goods inventory, and lower working capital requirements. Quality is higher and overall costs are lower. Indeed, even as sales are growing steadily, the company's return rate is only 6.8 percent, whereas most fashion brands have return rates as high as 40 percent—and that difference goes right to the company's bottom line.

RUFFWEAR: INCREASING FINANCIAL FLEXIBILITY

Many smaller companies that can't afford to set up offices internationally sell their products through distributors. The distributor buys the inventory from the company and then uses its people to sell the products (along with other products in the same or related categories) to retailers in that country. This arrangement allows small companies to generate revenue from around the world, even if they can't afford the expense of setting up offices and hiring staff internationally. For a company with this kind of relationship, the distributor becomes one of its most important customers.

Ruffwear, an Oregon-based company, designs and builds gear that allows dogs to join their owners on outdoor excursions—including packs for them to carry their own food, boots to protect their feet from sharp rocks, and even life jackets (!) to keep them safe on canoe or kayak trips. Like most outdoor industry companies, Ruffwear generally builds and sells products in two seasonal batches. (This makes sense—although dogs are happy to go outside any time of year, most dog owners confine their outdoor adventures to the summer and fall.) The company uses independent sales reps in the United States, but it sells in Europe through a distributor.

The twice-yearly batches of product posed a financial difficulty for the company's distributor. To keep shipping costs to a minimum, it would buy a full container of new product from Vietnam so that it could have inventory to sell at once, and additional inventory to replenish retailers' shelves during the course of the season. Financially, the inventory was like the proverbial pig in a python: a giant bulge of products that consumed an enormous amount of the distributor's cash, making it difficult to pay Ruffwear for the goods in a timely fashion, to say nothing of having money to spend on marketing and promotions.

The huge batch of inventory created another problem as well: with so much inventory in stock, the distributor would have to close out the old products at a discount to make room for the next season's products. This meant that Ruffwear's new products had to compete with its old, discounted products for space on the retailers' shelves. Alternatively, in order to get its new products into the market, Ruffwear had to buy back its old inventory from the distributor.

This dynamic is actually quite common in many industries, not just with industries that operate on a seasonal basis. Manufacturing and then holding too much product leads to endless discounts and sales, which hurt profitability for the manufacturer, the distributor, and the retailer alike. As Will Blount, the president of Ruffwear explains, "We have to realize that the *biggest waste* we create is manufacturing products that can't be sold for a healthy margin."

Blount, along with Young Joen, his director of supply chain, saw that this relationship with the distributor wasn't a recipe for growth in Europe. But rather than cutting costs at the head office, or negotiating harshly with his suppliers for better pricing, or pushing the distributor to bolster its financial reserves, the company decided to get fit—get faster and more agile in the way it worked with the distributor. First, it created greater visibility in its supply chain by investing in a centralized information system that provides the company with daily updates of actual sales and inventory levels. Next, it changed the way it shipped its products to Europe. In the past, it sent its products from Vietnam in standard cartons via ocean freight. This practice required the distributor to commit to which products it wanted four months in advance. Ruffwear switched to sending products from the United States in gaylord boxes via airfreight. This allowed the company to pack a mixed product assortment into a single box (which was much cheaper, given the company's soft and odd-sized products), and to deliver it significantly faster—five days in transit, instead of four weeks. Finally, Ruffwear ended the practice of delivering an entire season's worth of products in one shipment. Instead, it sent much smaller batches of product as often as twice per week.

The benefits from these changes were enormous. The distributor's cash flow improved because its money wasn't tied up in a huge batch of inventory. It was able to order products more accurately because it didn't have to forecast four months in advance. Smaller shipments also lowered logistics costs: the distributor uses a third-party warehouse that charges by the cubic meter. With less inventory on hand, storage costs were lower.

Naturally, the benefits accrued to Ruffwear as well. Accounts receivable declined by 62 percent. Closeouts went from 5.8 percent of total unit sales per year to 1.4 percent, meaning that the company didn't have to compete with its own discounted products when introducing new items. Taken together, these changes enabled the company to lower retail prices for its products in Europe by 7 percent—and still increase profits.

Blount sums up the benefits of organizational fitness elegantly:

> We want to build a reactive system that can take advantage of market conditions. Although we have a higher salary-to-revenue ratio than most other outdoor companies, the ratios of our other expenses to revenue are lower than those other firms. We take the savings from operation efficiency and invest in people.

These three examples demonstrate that a focus on increasing value for customers can yield even greater benefits than merely focusing on cost reduction. Cost cutting leads only to short-term benefits, with no long-term gain in skills or capability. By contrast, a value focus forces an organization to examine and improve its processes—making them faster, easier, safer, and higher quality. A cost-cutting focus puts the emphasis on financial results. A value focus puts the emphasis on process, which increases customer satisfaction and delivers long-term, sustainable benefits to the organization.

MONDAY MORNING TO-DO LIST

Here are some considerations to shift from cost cutting to value-adding efforts.

- What cost-reduction initiatives do you have underway now? Why did you target these areas?
- Talk to your marketing, sales, and customer service teams. What customer needs are not currently being met? Is your

organization falling short in terms of quality, availability, or support? List these opportunities. These are the gaps that you need to close.

- Bring your frontline and middle management workers together to figure out how to close these gaps to produce the end results you're looking for. (Remember: it's leadership's job to identify these gaps and decide which ones to address. It's the role of middle management and frontline workers to figure out how to do it.) Use coaching, visual management, and standard work to help workers reach these new targets.

- What key performance indicators can you create to enable you to track the improvements your team is making? These KPIs should be focused on *how* your processes operate rather than on your month-end financial results. Some examples:

  - Process productivity (labor hours per unit)
  - Number of items in a backlog queue
  - Percentage of forms filled out completely and accurately
  - Length of time to respond to customer inquiries
  - Number of incoming customer help desk calls (by product or service)
  - Customer satisfaction ratings

3

Think Horizontally

*O*rganizations are typically divided into functional silos: finance, marketing, sales, operations, and so on. There's nothing inherently wrong with this structure, but it increases the risk that the people and the departments within the company will focus on improving their own, internally directed metrics at the expense of the customer. It would be like a baseball player focusing on his home run tally at the expense of his team's ultimate World Series victory, or like a marathon runner focusing on how much he can bench press and not how fast he can cover the distance. This internal orientation is the natural default of all organizations, a combination of human desire for immediate rewards and evidence of success as well as natural organizational metabolism. Fit organizations, on the other hand, keep the customer in mind at all times—everything is viewed through the lens of the customer's perspective. That can be accomplished by a total reorganization of the way the company is organized, or it can be done by appointing a person to watch over the entire process by which the company creates value. Regardless of how you approach it, it's a shift that is essential to creating a fit organization.

Most organizations, and the people in them, spend an obscene amount of their time, energy, and resources working and fighting for the wrong things. They succumb to the natural default of organizational life where salespeople do what it takes to win bonuses, supply chain experts beat up vendors for pennies, workers behave to avoid punishment, and departments hunker down into their safe silos, walled off from the customer by their internally facing performance measurements. It's often a wonder that anyone shows initiative or spontaneity in delivering value for the customer.

Think about how you start a fitness program. Before beginning, you have (or should have) a goal. Are you trying to run a marathon, or are you trying to improve your tennis game? Do you want to build muscle or cardiovascular endurance? Are you trying to prevent a chronic knee injury from coming back, or do you just want to look better in a bathing suit this summer? These questions are critical to determining what specific exercises, and what kind of fitness routine, you'll pursue.

Different goals necessitate different training regimens. Running the Boston Marathon requires stamina and lower body muscular endurance, whereas doing a 5K race places a greater premium on speed and cardiovascular capacity. And of course, any sort of running event requires a completely different kind of fitness than a tennis match, which demands agility, flexibility, quickness, and a fair amount of upper body strength.

Now, most people intuitively understand the need to orient their workouts toward their specific athletic or fitness goal. You don't see too many people doing a set of 400-meter sprints on the track to improve their golf game, or doing a bunch of bicep curls with heavy weights to prepare for a marathon. Why? Because your mile time doesn't correlate well with your ability to get out of a sand trap, and your bicep girth isn't going to help you at Heartbreak Hill in the Boston Marathon.

However, we don't carry that mindset over to the business world. Irrespective of the industry we're in, the type of products or services we provide, or the kind of customers we serve, our businesses are organized into pretty much the same kind of functional silos—sales, marketing, finance, product development, customer service, HR, IT, and so on. For example, Figure 3.1 shows what silos might look like in product development:

FIGURE 3.1 Silos in product development.

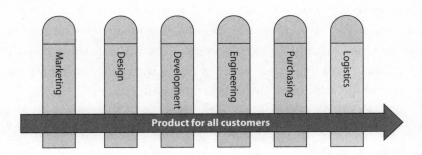

Of course, there's nothing inherently wrong with an organization built around functional silos. But that structure has a real and significant consequence, because the siloed organizational chart profoundly shapes our thinking. It pulls workers' focus away from the customer's needs (either customers in another department, or the ultimate consumer) and shifts it internally toward the department's needs. The silo mentality causes people to think more about what's best for their department than about what's best for their customer. Put another way, it makes people think "vertically" instead of "horizontally."

This shift in thinking leads ineluctably to suboptimization of organizational processes. Departments within a company concentrate on improving metrics related to their specific domain, rather than on improving the customer experience. For example, in most companies, customer service departments are evaluated on how fast reps are able to end phone calls. Shorter phone calls means that the company needs fewer people to answer the phones—which means lower costs in the department. Some companies also argue that shorter calls mean happier customers because questions are being answered more expeditiously (although most of us would argue that this is pretty shaky ground to stand on). In fact, there's a host of software applications that slice and dice call center data to help managers figure out how to "improve"— that is, reduce—the amount of time spent on the phone. In many other companies, customer service is outsourced to India or some other low-wage country in order to reduce department costs, even if that results in lower levels of service. It's a rare person who hasn't had a painful experience with a rep whose English is difficult to understand, who reads off a script that bears little relevance to the customer's situation or mood, and who seems more interested in getting the customer off the phone quickly rather than in resolving his or her problem.

What's missing from this vertical, silo-focused analysis, of course, is customer satisfaction. Reducing the average time per call or overall department expenses may be good for department metrics, but it doesn't necessarily improve the quality of the service that the customer receives. In contrast to this silo-focused thinking and measurement, online retailer Zappos doesn't care at all how long reps spend on the phone with customers. Zappos is horizontally oriented, completely focused on the customer experience. The company's first core value is "Deliver WOW through service"—and embracing that value gives the customer service team license to spend however much time and money that demands. (In 2012, the company set an internal record with a 10-hour, 29-minute phone call.) Or consider the legendary "empty chair" at Amazon. CEO Jeff Bezos includes an empty chair in important meetings with his senior leaders to remind everyone of the most important person to the company: the customer. The chair encourages attendees to think of their proposals and ideas through the customer's eyes—what would she think? How would she react? Assessing your products, your services, and your work through the customer's eyes: this is a pretty simple idea. And yet it typically gets lost in the daily activities of most organizations when they're focused inward, toward the top of their functional silos.

Fujitsu Services, an IT service company, embraced this shift to customer orientation in a deep, systemic fashion. Facing stiff competition, customer dissatisfaction, and high levels of employee turnover, the company fundamentally restructured the way it provided service to its clients. Efficiency—an internal metric—was no longer the primary score. (The company continued to track call duration and total number of calls, but that was only to ensure correct staffing levels.) Instead, the focus shifted to "customer success" and satisfaction. Frontline call center staff were given responsibility for identifying product and process improvements that customers needed. They visited customer sites to better understand their working environment, and they developed customer-specific key performance indicators. They even provided advice to customers on how they could improve their own suboptimal processes. Fujitsu's managers' roles changed, too. Rather than using their authority to ensure worker compliance with internal policies and procedures, they took on a support role in which their primary responsibility was to provide frontline staff with the necessary knowledge and tools to handle the needs of the customer and assume responsibility for end-to-end service. These changes drove 20 percent higher customer satisfaction rates, improved employee satisfaction by 40 percent, reduced attrition from 42 percent to 8 percent, and lowered operating costs by 20 percent.[1]

Siloed thinking doesn't just affect entry-level jobs like customer service. For example, hospital-based physicians are under continual pressure to increase patient throughput, which means spending less time with each patient. "Optimizing" the way that doctors spend their time in the exam room may increase hospital revenue and reduce the need to hire additional physicians (at least in the short term), but it doesn't necessarily provide patients with the best care.

You would never use a single workout regimen for all your fitness goals; you would design it to meet a specific objective. Just like a fitness program needs to be oriented toward a specific goal—running a marathon, rehabbing a specific injury, playing better tennis—a fit organization orients around the customer and her needs. A fit organization thinks horizontally, not vertically.

THE PERILS OF VERTICAL THINKING

Call centers are a particularly egregious example of how silo thinking hurts the customer experience. But siloed organizations also tend to struggle with internecine battles caused by poorly aligned incentives. For example, one of the core measures of performance in a credit department is the number of "days sales outstanding," or DSOs. This metric shows how long it takes customers to pay their bills. The finance and accounting department doesn't like it when DSOs increase, because the longer it takes to collect on open invoices, the more likely it is that the customer won't pay at all. If the DSOs for a customer—or more important, a group of customers—get too high, the credit department will put the customer on credit hold and refuse to ship merchandise. From a strictly financial perspective, this makes sense. But certain types of customers have different sales rates—a major retailer like Foot Locker can move product more quickly and pay bills sooner than the neighborhood triathlon shop. Holding these two types of accounts to the same payment standards will inevitably result in slower sales (and a frustrated sales force).

Siloed metrics such as DSOs destroy intracompany teamwork as well. The financial executive is measured and rewarded in part on reducing DSOs, which leads her to tighten credit. By contrast, the sales executive is measured and rewarded on increased sales volume, which leads him to create dating programs that increase the DSOs. (Wiremold, a manufacturer of cable management equipment, solved this problem by tying incentive compensation for all high-level executives around the world to the same metrics—which were based on worldwide results.)

Vertical thinking also increases the likelihood of errors. Each time information passes from one silo to another, there's a handoff—from sales to customer service, from product marketing to design, or from development to purchasing. Whenever you separate knowledge, responsibility, action, and feedback, you're inviting disaster, because decisions are being made by people who don't have enough knowledge to make them well.[2] Not only that: despite the ubiquity of email and an overabundance of meetings, communication between and among teams of adults isn't too far removed from the children's game of telephone. Even with workers' full focus and the best of intentions, messages get garbled when they're passed from silo to silo. Most people reading this book have probably experienced a moment when they (or someone in their organization) said, "When did we agree to *that*?"

Vertical organization also slows companies down. Workers spend an enormous amount of time preparing PowerPoint presentations, writing memos, or simply sitting in meetings briefing people in the next department about what's happening. Of course, none of this time and effort is value added from the customer's perspective. It's simply a necessary cost of doing business when work is flowing across departmental boundaries. Even worse, when work is handed off between functions, it almost always goes into some sort of queue, so the next person (or step) in the process has to wait until the preceding person does his job. The delays caused by these queues can be enormous.

Bison Gear & Engineering Corporation, a manufacturer of custom electric motors and gearmotors near Chicago, struggled with precisely this problem. Handoffs between designers, electrical engineers, and mechanical engineers led to a three-week lead time for new product development. In their market, three weeks just wasn't good enough, and they were losing business to competitors. Bison responded by breaking down the silos between these departments in what they call a "project blitz." The company puts a team of engineers together (literally—they move their desks right next to each other), protects them from interruptions by stretching police riot tape across the engineers' area so that no one can enter, and has them focus exclusively on a single project until it's completed. Work flows smoothly and continuously from one person to another with no waiting and no distractions. Also no memos, no presentations, and no meetings. The lead time to produce a custom motor now? Three days.

A Better Alternative: Horizontal Orientation

A fit organization focuses horizontally, toward the customer, resulting in higher quality, better service, faster response, and happier customers. Going back to the athletic metaphor, this is equivalent to planning a workout regimen with a specific event in mind, rather than focusing on individual muscle groups without consideration for the ultimate training goal. Horizontal orientation enables—even encourages—the company to optimize its activities for the benefit of the customer, and not the department manager or VP.

A company that thinks horizontally considers the types of customers it serves and breaks them down by their different needs (see Figure 3.2). For a consumer products company, that could mean domestic vs. international customers. For a law firm, it could be corporate vs. individual clients. For a hospital, it might be cancer patients vs. trauma victims. Each of these customer types has different product and service requirements, which can be best addressed by the creation of separate processes tailored to their needs.

Despite the advantages and intuitive logic of orienting around customer types, disbanding functional silos is a heavy lift for most organizations. More than a century of business tradition has led to the primacy of silos. This history, combined with the legacy of Frederick Taylor's principles of scientific management (which argue for work specialization), makes it exceedingly difficult to orient in any other way. Additionally, most metrics and key performance indicators (KPIs) point vertically—time spent on a call in a customer service center; days sales outstanding in the credit department; commission percentage in sales; viewing only unit cost, rather than total cost, of a product in purchasing; and so on—which makes it all the more difficult to focus on the customer. Even when a company does have an internal advocate for the customer, all too often that person doesn't have the formal authority or informal clout to change the decisions made by functional VPs.

FIGURE 3.2 Horizontal orientation by customer type.

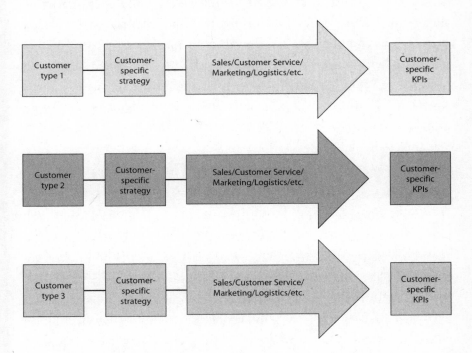

Nevertheless, it's possible to bring the benefits of horizontal orientation to an organization that maintains its functional departments.

Asics

In 1992, Asics, the athletic footwear company, was on a roll. Over the previous four years, the U.S. subsidiary of this Japanese firm nearly tripled revenue to $250 million, primarily by increasing volume in large chains like Foot Locker and Footaction. At the same time, however, sales through the specialty running channel suffered. Asics slipped from the top spot in this channel to number three. And although the sales volume from running specialty retailers accounted for only about 5 percent of the company's business, these shops were critical to Asics' brand image. For my first job out of business school, I was hired to fix this situation.

In talking with the specialty running accounts, I learned that they were leaving Asics for competitors like Saucony and Brooks because the company wasn't serving their particular needs. Policies, processes, and systems that worked for chains with 1,000 storefronts that ordered 40,000 pairs of shoes at a time didn't work for a single operator that ordered 72 pairs at a time. Figuring out how to work around the company's functional silos to better serve these retailers was the challenge.

Special Needs

Big chain stores are sophisticated operations that manage their cash and inventory professionally. (Generally speaking. Lord knows that there are plenty of chains that struggle to do so.) Foot Locker, for example, places all its orders before the season starts, schedules delivery throughout the season to refill its stocks, and strategically holds extra inventory at its distribution centers as needed. It pays its bills on time, and when it has a problem, its sales clout gets it fast attention from a vendor's customer service and leadership teams.

Small running shops are entirely different. They're run on a tight budget—and that's when the owner is sophisticated enough to even have a budget. In the 1980s and '90s in particular, many of them were operated as a labor of love by serious runners who knew more about mile splits than about income statements. The owners were often disorganized and didn't have a lot of cash to pay bills (when they could find them in the chaos of their desks), which landed the stores on credit hold with their vendors. Being cash poor also meant that they couldn't buy a lot of inventory. As a result, they lived in fear of stocking out of a shoe in a customer's size (if you lose a customer today, he'll probably go to Foot Locker, and the sale will be gone forever), leading them to rely on vendors to carry enough inventory to "fill in" their stock with overnight shipments. By 1992, the Asics functionally oriented organization was terrific at meeting the needs of large chains, and terrible at meeting the needs of the small guys—and that's why the running shops fled to Saucony and Brooks. Those smaller competitors had less business with the giant chains and could—or at least chose to—pay more attention to the running shops.

End-to-End Service Focused on One Type of Customer

I realized that for Asics to address the different needs of the running specialty shop, virtually every department in the company had to reconsider the way they operated and the way they measured their performance. They needed to orient their services around these accounts.

> *Sales.* Discounts are typically given to customers based on volume. Running specialty accounts can't get those discounts because they can't order enough products to meet the threshold. We created unique discount levels based on their smaller size (for example, 72 pairs of shoes, not 288 pairs). We developed specific sales programs and incentives for them if they would carry one additional SKU or increase an order of a particular model from 24 pairs to 36. Finally, to help them with their cash flow, we gave them special terms

and dating: instead of Net 60 days, we went to Net 90 on "futures" orders and Net 60 on "fill-in" orders.

Credit. By any measure, most running specialty accounts are terrible credit risks compared to large chains or mass merchants. Nevertheless, we changed the threshold at which these accounts would be put on credit hold, and we allowed them to pay off their outstanding invoices more slowly than other accounts. The credit department even segregated these accounts when calculating overall Days Sales Outstanding (DSO) metrics.

Customer service. Because prompt customer service is essential to these accounts, and because they rely more on the customer service department, we formed a special team of customer service reps that handled only running specialty stores. When the customer service reps had free time, they would make outbound calls to the stores to check on inventory, place additional orders, and deal with any problems they had. Reps on this team weren't evaluated on average call length.

Purchasing. Like most companies, Asics tended to have plenty of inventory of the shoes no one wanted and never enough inventory of the shoes that were in high demand. That made retailers reluctant to rely on Asics too heavily because the company often couldn't provide fill-in orders. To allay their fears, we created a shoe bank each season that held extra stock of the "meat sizes" (8, 9, 10, and 11) of two core models. This bank was reserved for the exclusive use of the specialty running shops—no other class of retailer could poach from it.

Shipping. Specialty running shops hated competing with the big chains. The big guys would often discount shoes by five to ten dollars to get customers in the doors—a discount that the running shops, with their thinner margins, couldn't match. To help them compete better, Asics began shipping one key running model to these stores a month before the big chains got it. That gave them one month of selling without major competition.

Promotions. Big chains have their own marketing budgets, or they extract marketing money from their vendors. Specialty running shops can't match that. We increased the level of sponsorship for store-based running clubs with free and discounted products, as well as races that stores organized in their communities. We also provided low-cost running accessories (socks, T-shirts, etc.) to specialty retailers that increased their orders to certain thresholds.

Metrics. To emphasize the new horizontal focus on this specific customer, Asics abolished most of the internal departmental metrics related to them—and when they were maintained, like DSOs or inventory cost of the product in the shoe bank, they were calculated separately. We also added an overall satisfaction metric for the running specialty program as a whole and tracked sales through this distribution channel in aggregate, and the sales per storefront.

The results: Within one year, Asics recaptured the top position within this distribution channel, a position it held for the next 19 years.

Menlo Innovations

Rich Sheridan started Menlo Innovations, a software development company in Ann Arbor, with the intent of bringing joy (yes, joy) back to software. He wanted to build a company that was a joyful place to work, with the intention that a joyful culture would create solid software that was a joy to use.

Sheridan's long experience in the industry showed him that working in most software companies was like being in a salt mine, with executives flogging programmers through a coding death march to meet delivery deadlines; quality assurance staff trying to convince programmers that the bugs they find are real and need to be fixed—and after they fail, product managers trying to convince the sales team that those bugs are actually value-added features; and the documentation team laboring over manuals that no one will ever read. Okay—this description may be slightly hyperbolic. Not all software projects are that painful. But you can be sure that Healthcare.gov and Windows Vista (perhaps the largest software project failure in history, estimated at over $10B spent for a product that everyone hated and was killed as soon as possible) must have been pretty close to this level of dysfunction.

Sheridan realized that one of the primary causes of these problems was the traditional silo-based approach to software development. Here's an overview of how a traditional software development company operates compared to the way Menlo does it:

Traditional Software Companies	The Menlo Innovations Way
Programming. Separate silo, and usually specialized by coding language. Often outsourced. Language, culture, and time zone differences complicate the handoff of work within and between functional groups.	*Programming.* Integrated into a larger project team. Always code in pairs. No technical specialties.
Business analysis/project management. Separate silos. Both functions are part of other silos such as marketing or finance. Communication with programming mostly occurs through reams of mandatory documentation.	*Business analysis/project management.* None. "High-tech Anthropologists®" are responsible for understanding the customer's business goals and the user's need through interviews, on-site observations, and low-tech prototyping of software designs.

Traditional Software Companies	The Menlo Innovations Way
Designers. Separate silo. Not deeply invested in any particular customer. Often force a particular design to create an arbitrary consistency among unrelated projects. Also tend to follow industry norms for user experiences.	*Designers.* Incorporated in the programming team. Work closely with the High-tech Anthropologists.
Quality assurance. Separate silo. Often outsourced offshore. Disdained by programmers. Works on software after it has all been written.	*Quality assurance.* QA members are an integral part of the team. Quality is built in at all stages of the project with automated test units. Clients check usability weekly.
Documentation. Separate silo. Comes in after the software is done.	*Documentation.* Incorporated in the project team.
Other departments. Separate silos. Brought in for specific needs. A separate team almost always needed for after-sale support and emergency fixes.	*Other departments.* Either included in the project team, such as infrastructure, or not needed at all, like after-sale support (see below).
Key performance metrics. Almost exclusively internally focused: expense per hour, number of hours per person; adherence to budget; adherence to spec.	*Key performance metrics.* Customer joy. (Seriously.)

Here's a more detailed description of the differences in the way a typical software company works versus Menlo Innovations.

Programming. For cost reasons, many companies have outsourced their software development team to an offshore service provider in, say, Chennai, with management by the internal IT team in the United States. Needless to say, the language, culture, and time zone differences massively complicate the handoff of work within and between functional silos. There are even silos within the silo, as programmers are usually organized into towers of knowledge: database experts, low-level programmers, middleware experts, frameworks experts, application programming interface (API) architects and developers, and front-end developers. There's typically a very strong technology bent to everyone on this team—in Sheridan's words, "almost a religious fervor." This is why you see programmers self-identify by a specific technology. For example, people will say, "I am a Ruby on Rails developer," or "I'm a Microsoft.NET programmer," or "I'm an Oracle 9.1.1.3 SP2 expert." None of these people can do anything outside their tower of knowledge, meaning that projects are always at risk of delay if someone gets sick, goes on vacation, or leaves the company.

Business analysis/project management. This function is supposed to ensure that the project both is valuable for the company and is running on time, although developers usually override the business analyst when there's a conflict. The business analyst is typically part of another functional area such as product management and reports up through marketing or a functional business unit. Analysts produce customer-use cases and fill out reams of forms stipulated by the software development life cycle process. Of course, no one actually reads these forms during development, so they're of marginal utility (except to the QA department, which uses the documents later as a form of self-defense to justify why they're finding so many problems). Project management is the realm of the project management office (PMO). The PMO is usually part of the financial silo because it controls the budget for projects in each functional area. The PMO is a matrixed organization responsible to both the finance department and other functional areas.

Designers. The design team handles the front-end look and feel of software. It comprises wireframers (who mock up the layout of a screen or web page), to graphical user interface (GUI) designers, to graphic artists. They often fall victim to the siren call of consistency between unrelated products, because they work on a portfolio of projects for all types of customers.

Also, since they're not deeply invested in any particular customer, they often follow industry norms suggesting that there are right ways and wrong ways to build user experiences. *Quality assurance.* Despite the obvious importance to the customer of quality assurance, this silo doesn't get a lot of respect. Like many of the programmers, they're often located offshore. They start their work long after the software bugs have settled into concrete. Sheridan describes the relationship between QA and the developers this way:

> The QA team is usually sequestered in the basement of Building 3, far away from the programmers, as programmers are way too busy to trouble themselves with pesky details like "the software doesn't seem to work." The most typical response from programmers? "It worked on my machine."

Documentation. Their job is to fix the broken user experience through documentation they know in their hearts no one will ever read. (Really. Have you ever read a user manual?) *Other departments.* If there's a regulatory component (like the FDA), or specific security issues (such as software for credit card machines at a mass merchant like Target), more silos and vice presidents will inevitably be involved. If there is a large infrastructure component, then IT infrastructure will be another stakeholder. Finally, there's almost always a separate team that handles after-sale support and makes emergency software fixes for the customer.
Key performance metrics. KPIs for software companies are almost exclusively internally focused. They measure how much they spend per person per hour; the number of hours per person; whether or not they stayed within budget; and whether they built the software they had spec'd (irrespective

of whether or not it's really useful to the users). The most customer-focused metric is on-time delivery—and even that measurement largely points toward their internal performance.

The Menlo Way

The Menlo Innovations approach breaks down these silos and organizes entire project teams around the customer. Teams are cross-functional, including all skill sets needed to deliver a project on time and on budget. The company has done away with business analysts from another functional silo. Rather, their "High-tech Anthropologists®" are an essential part of the team, responsible for deeply understanding the customer's business goals and the user's need through interviews with the customer and anthropological discovery with the customer's users; on-site observations of users in their natural environments; and low-tech prototyping of software designs. Before the programmers even start coding, the project team understands how customers will use the software and is aligned and in agreement on what needs to be done.

To avoid the sub-silos that form around technical specialties, Menlo programmers don't specialize in any specific technology—all of them code in all languages. They also code in pairs, meaning that two people sit at one computer when programming—one person types, and the other reviews the code in real time. The keyboard moves freely back and forth between the pair. The pairs change regularly to ensure that knowledge, skills, and experiences are shared and transferred throughout the company.

Quality is built in at all stages of the project. Programmers write automated test units for their code before they even write the code itself to ensure that they don't "game" the test to fit the code they've written. Moreover, QA members are an integral part of the project team from the start, rather than coming in at the end. And clients come in for a weekly "show and tell" of the new code to ensure that it meets client expectations at all stages of development.

Menlo's primary metric is purely customer focused: it measures joy for the people it serves. (Seriously.) Of course, the company never meets the people it serves, and these people don't pay Menlo directly for the work the company does. Nevertheless, Menlo explicitly defines joy this way:

> Joy is delivering software to the world that delights the people who use it every day.

The company is even willing to build this metric right into its business contracts. It's willing to trade away a substantial amount of profit in exchange for equity in the client's company and royalty in the product it designs and builds. Menlo is willing to bet that a product or service that delights users will drive business results. In 2014, almost 15 percent of annual revenue came from royalties alone. Sheridan explains that this approach can actually cost the company business:

> Why would this philosophy get us in trouble with the clients who pay us to do this work? Because if the sponsor is focused on short-term rewards like cutting expenses, delivering quickly no matter what, looking good to their bosses even if they are building the wrong thing, our joyful focus becomes really annoying. Some even fire us for this myopic focus. We're OK with that.

The ultimate evidence that Menlo's approach works—in addition to profitable growth every year—is this: the phone (almost) never rings with customer problems. (In fact, I spent three hours there last winter, and there wasn't a single phone call.) Sheridan estimates that in 14 years of business, the company has had about five calls asking for assistance with serious problems. Five. Most software companies? They get hundreds of calls *per day* because of problems with their software.[1]

Some wonder if all this attention to joy and quality is worth it. For Sheridan and Menlo, the question isn't relevant regarding revenue or profit or growth. It is relevant to joy. Joy, both in the workplace and in the delight of providing an outstanding experience to the customers that use the work of Menlo's hearts, hands, and minds every day.

Aluminum Trailer Company

Based in Indiana, Aluminum Trailer Company (ATC) is a manufacturer of (you guessed it) aluminum trailers for more purposes than you can probably imagine. Their products include trailers designed for disaster response, mobile command, living quarters, and even food vending. And that doesn't even include the custom trailers it builds.

Until 2012, ATC was organized, like most companies, into functional silos—sales, design, engineering, manufacturing, customer service, finance, and so on. The silos didn't talk to each other very much, except to complain when one of the other functions wasn't responding fast enough to an email. In fact, people in the silos didn't even see each other very much—one of the salespeople discovered that it took her 101 steps to walk from her desk to the engineering department. That's about 80 to 100 yards (each way!) in a company with only 160 people.

Those long walks may have been good for exercise, but they weren't very good for business. Customer service suffered, with emails stacking up in inboxes for two or three days at a time without a response. (With a 200-yard round trip, people didn't eagerly race across the building to follow up on a message.) The silos also created an "us versus them" mentality between departments, with plenty of finger-pointing and blame when there was a problem or something needed to be redone. Perhaps most perniciously, the siloed approach led people to work more slowly. CEO Steve Brenneman explains it this way:

> When people are physically separated and vertically oriented, they can't see what's happening in other departments. Let's say you're a highly skilled engineer who works fast. You don't know what the designers or salespeople are dealing with. You just know that there's not a lot of work for you to do

right now, so you take it easy and work more slowly. But if you knew what they were working on, you might be able to help them. Or you might be able to get a jump on the work that will be coming to you in a week, rather than waiting for the tsunami to overwhelm you later.

One final problem with ATC's vertical orientation was that it didn't learn from previous work. By treating all types of customer orders the same, and by not sharing information across the functional departments, the company couldn't create "reusable knowledge." Brenneman jokes,

> We didn't build trailers; we built snowflakes. We treated every trailer as a one-of-a-kind order. We hoped that the customer would never order that trailer twice, because then we'd have to discover how to do it all over again.

The New Way: Three Types of Customers, Three Teams

To reduce the number of errors and the amount of time it took to deliver a trailer, Brenneman completely eliminated the departmental silos and reorganized the company horizontally into "value streams"[2] around three types of customers. "Value Stream 1" serves customers who want an off-the-rack trailer that requires no (or minimal) changes. "Value Stream 2" serves customers who need slight modifications and tailoring. And "Value Stream 3," staffed with the most skilled people, serves customers who demand fully customized, highly complex products. (Brenneman somewhat sheepishly acknowledges that these aren't exactly the most creative names for the teams.)

Each team is made up of a coordinator, salespeople, designers, and engineers. In contrast to the vast physical (and psychological) distances between silos in the old organization, everyone in the value stream sits together, with no walls between members of the team. An internal salesperson on each team coordinates the internal activities needed to generate a price quote for a product and get customer approval. Each team is focused exclusively on one particular type of customer, which means that they're able to capture and reuse knowledge. (No more snowflakes.) The physical proximity reduces delays when handing off work between people and has completely eliminated the "us versus them" mentality that accompanies vertical thinking and silos. Figure 3.3 shows the team in Value Stream 2.

FIGURE 3.3 Value Stream 2 team.

Finance and R&D still exist as separate departments that provide shared services to the three teams. In finance, the company has no choice, because there are only two people who have the necessary skills. Even though R&D stands alone as a department, it doesn't get overloaded (like the R&D team at Vaisala, which I'll describe in Chapter 5) because the company holds regular meetings with all three teams and the R&D group to agree on priorities.

How has the change worked out? Since implementing this new organizational structure, ATC has improved productivity (revenue per man-hour) by 11 percent per year. It also turns around orders faster: it used to take about seven weeks to get ready for an order and one week to make it. Now it only takes two weeks to prep for an order and one week to build it.

Notwithstanding these financial benefits, Brenneman says the most valuable benefit of ATC's horizontal value stream management is that the end customer is now visible and connected to the whole team at ATC. In the past, only the salespeople knew the customer—office and plant personnel had no connection to their users. Now, everyone sitting in the value streams is doing value-added work for the end customer. His ultimate goal is to have everyone sitting or functioning within the value streams they've set up. Faster service, better internal dynamics, fewer errors, higher productivity—what's not to like?

Fitness programs must be tailored to your specific objectives, or you'll waste time and energy and fail utterly to reach your goals. In the same way, your organization must be oriented around the specific needs and wants of your customers. Your functional departments must measure and design their work to serve specific customers, not their own internal needs. After all, it's the customer who keeps score—not the department VP. How are you going to satisfy that scorekeeper?

MONDAY MORNING TO-DO LIST

Here are some steps that will help you shift from a vertically oriented organization built around departments to a horizontally oriented one built around the customer.

- List your major customer types and points of differentiation. Think about differences in size, geography, and distribution channels. Consider how, when, and where they use your products or services.

- Interview representative customers for each type. What do they value most? Why? Compare these answers across the different types you've identified.
- Interview people (both VPs and frontline workers) in your functional departments. What specific needs or challenges do they deal with when working with these different customer types?
- Examine everything you do in each major process through the filter of whether it serves the customer or your own internally focused metrics. What waste can you see? How can you shift focus from working vertically to working horizontally?
- Create three to five metrics that reflect what's important for each customer type. (In general, these metrics will be holistic and won't tie into the metrics you use for your internal measurements.)
- Create a "value stream manager" for each customer type. The value stream manager's responsibility is to advocate for the customer, not the departmental head. Remember, you don't have to go as far as Menlo Innovations or Aluminum Trailer and completely get rid of silos. Asics maintained its functional silos but gave me authority and responsibility to advocate for one type of customer. Note that if your customer base doesn't break naturally into customer types, you may benefit from creating value streams around product families. (For example, if you're a manufacturer with production split among multiple plants, it may make sense to organize around product families.)

4

Standard Work

"Standard work" is the foundation for improvement. It represents the current understanding of the best way, or the "right way," to work, and in so doing allows for comparison with new approaches and techniques. Standard work is not devised and imposed by leaders or managers. Rather, it's developed by the people who are actually doing the job—after all, no one has a better understanding of how things really work than they do. An added benefit is that it generates shared knowledge, as workers within departments cooperate and communicate to define the best way to work. Leaders need standard work, too. It ensures predictability and consistency of action, prevents important issues from falling through the cracks, and is a powerful tool to pull leaders out of their offices so that they can see how the organization operates on a daily basis. Employee coaching and development should always be built into a leader's standard work.

If you're serious about pursuing physical fitness, you need to work out correctly. To do that, you should have some knowledge of anatomy, physiology, and biomechanics. You should also understand how the body responds both to stress and to rest. And while you're at it, it wouldn't be a bad idea to know something about nutrition and diet. Of course, if you don't spend your nights poring over *Muscle & Fitness* or *Shape* magazine and haven't acquired all this information, you hire a trainer. A good trainer oversees each individual exercise to ensure that you get maximum benefits while avoiding injury. The trainer also supervises you over the long term to ensure that you build strength and fitness without breaking down. In short, the trainer isn't there just to look good in spandex (although there's certainly nothing wrong with having that motivational sight). The trainer is there to show you the right way to train and help you achieve maximal results.

Consider the case of Tom Brady, the quarterback for the New England Patriots. Brady is unquestionably one of the greatest football players of all time (and as a lifelong New York Jets fan, growing up in a family of Jets fans, you have no idea how much it pains me to admit that). Brady is also remarkably durable: aside from losing a full season for knee surgery, he's missed only one game during his 15-year career. Yes, he's talented. Yes, he's surrounded by skilled players who both protect him and catch his passes. Undoubtedly, he's lucky as well. But Brady's success is also due to an unbelievably methodical, structured approach to skill development and physical fitness. A recent profile explains Brady's process this way:

> Brady is a quarterback whose daily schedule, both in and out of season, is mapped clearly into his 40s. Every day of it, micromanaged. Treatment. Workouts. Food. Recovery. Practice. Rest. And those schedules aren't just for this week, this month, this season. They're for three years. That allows Brady and [Alex] Guerrero [Brady's body coach] to work in both the short and long terms to, say, increase muscle mass one year and focus on pliability the next. "The whole idea is to program his body to do what we want it to do," says Guerrero. "We don't let the body dictate to us. We dictate. Everything is calculated."
>
> . . . The in-season portion of his regimen is designed to run through Super Bowl Sunday; if New England's campaign ends in a playoff loss . . . , Brady completes every drill, every throw, anyway.

That's their system. From the outset the principles made sense to Brady, who had spent the early part of his career like most athletes. He'd worried about injuries after they happened. He'd focused on rehabilitation as opposed to preventative maintenance.

. . . The week after the Patriots fell to the Ravens in the 2013 AFC Championship Game, Brady showed up for workouts with his trainer, Gunnar Peterson, a Band-Aid still on his arm from some game scrape. "This guy is year-round," says Peterson. . . . "No wasted movement. No plays off. No days off. Everything is purposeful." [1]

If you're following a training schedule for some event, you know that the overall arc of your workouts is carefully designed to get you ready to compete at the right time. If you're Tom Brady, you have a comprehensive schedule for all your exercises, drills, and throws. If you're training for a marathon, there's a steady ramp-up in mileage, culminating in one or two 20-mile runs, before you begin your final taper. You don't just run a random distance based on how you feel that day or how much time you have ("Hey, it's a nice afternoon and the kids are away— I think I'll go for 20."), any more than Brady just decides to do a bunch of bench presses because he feels good. Do your 20-miler too early, and you'll get injured; do it too late, and you won't recover for the race. There's a cadence that you need to follow for optimum performance.

Does this discipline and structure sound extreme? Perhaps. But as James Surowiecki explains,

It's how you end up with someone like Chris Hoy, the British cyclist who won two gold medals at the London Olympics in 2012, trailed by a team of scientists, nutritionists, and engineers. Hoy ate a carefully designed diet of five thousand calories a day. His daily workouts—two hours of lifting in the morning, three hours in the velodrome in the afternoon, and an easy one-hour recovery ride in the evening—had been crafted to maximize both his explosive power and his endurance. He had practiced in wind tunnels at the University of Southampton. He had worn biofeedback sensors that delivered exact data to his trainers about how his body was responding to practice. The eighty-thousand-dollar carbon-fiber bike he rode helped, too. Hoy was the ultimate product of an elaborate and finely tuned system designed to create the best cyclist possible. And—since his competitors weren't slacking, either—he still won by only a fraction of a second.[2]

If you want to build and lead a fit organization, you have to bring this kind of focused discipline to activities on both the organizational and the personal level. It's the basis for all improvement.

Now, it's true that leading an organization, or even just a team of people, is far more complex than getting fit, or training for a marathon, or even quarterbacking a professional football team. Sure, there's some unpredictability in training—you might get sick, or twist an ankle, or you might be trapped at a weeklong family event with your crazy grandmother in Slippery Rock (in August!) that makes training all but impossible—but by and large, it's pretty easy to follow a plan if you're disciplined.

Let's call this plan, on both the micro and the macro level, "standard work." Standard work in an organization is the baseline against which any modifications are compared to see if there's been improvement. It's like the control group in a medical experiment: it's the thing that stays constant so that you can see whether or not the new surgical technique is an improvement over the old approach. Standard work represents the best (easiest, fastest, least expensive, highest-quality) way we know to do something, whether that's hitting a seven iron, doing a clean-and-jerk, processing an invoice, or coaching an employee on problem-solving techniques. When people don't (or can't) follow the standard work, that's a clear problem, a gap between what they should do and what they actually do. That gap is a signal that there's an opportunity for improvement in how the system functions—or an opportunity to create a new standard that delivers even higher-quality work with less effort.

TRAINING WITHIN INDUSTRY

Most people know the legend of Rosie the Riveter. During World War II, when 12 million working-aged men served in the United States armed forces, women were essential to keeping the American war machine—the "arsenal of democracy"—running. In 1943, some 310,000 women worked in the U.S. aircraft industry, making up 65 percent of the industry's total workforce. By 1944, more than four million women worked in the defense industry overall.[3]

But consider for a minute what was required to convert four million homemakers and pink-collar workers into skilled mechanics, technicians, and, well, riveters. Assembling a B-24 bomber is quite a bit more complicated and difficult than baking an apple pie. (Although a really good apple pie isn't easy, either.) And the downside consequences of poor construction in a B-24 were significantly higher than a soggy piecrust. The forgotten secret behind this remarkable transformation of the American workforce was Training Within Industry.

The U.S. government created the Training Within Industry (TWI) program during World War II to support the war production effort. Millions of civilians—not just women—needed to be quickly trained to do production jobs as soldiers went off to war. The program was directed at both supervisors and frontline workers, and it led to astonishing improvements in quality, safety, productivity, and cost:

- Eighty-six percent of the companies increased production by 25 percent or more.
- All companies reduced training time by 25 percent or more.
- Eighty-eight percent of the companies reduced labor hours by 25 percent or more.
- Fifty-five percent of the companies reduced scrap by 25 percent or more.
- All companies reduced grievances by 25 percent or more.[4]

After the war ended, the U.S. government used TWI to help rebuild Japan's infrastructure, which was utterly destroyed during the war. TWI was also widely adopted by leading Japanese companies in the postwar era, even as it was being forgotten at home in the United States. In a nearly unbelievable ironic twist, TWI fell so deeply into the dustbin of the collective American industrial memory that it was perceived as a *Japanese* quality program when it was reintroduced to the United States by consultants and Japanese companies in the 1980s and 1990s.

The power of TWI rests on the belief that there is a *right* way for individuals to do their work and a *right* way for supervisors to manage people and teach their staff how to do their work correctly—whether that's riveting a piece of sheet metal onto an airplane wing or mixing the ingredients for a batch of Froot Loops. This belief is manifested in the four areas of TWI: job relations, job instructions, job methods, and job safety.

- *Job relations:* teaches supervisors how to manage people effectively.
- *Job instructions:* teaches supervisors how to break down a job into its component parts and teach them to another person.
- *Job methods:* teaches supervisors how to analyze the elements of a job and improve them.
- *Job safety:* teaches supervisors how to instruct employees in preventive measures that reduce accidents and injuries.

It's important to mention that the right way to work isn't immutable, handed down from the mountain and chiseled into granite, shackling people to an unchanging standard. The right way to work is based on current knowledge and understanding—but if conditions change, or if people come up with better ways to do the work, then the right way to work changes. Freestyle swimmers, for example, were once taught to pull their arms through the water in an "S" pattern. Today, however, swimmers pull their arms straight back. In track and field, high jumpers historically went over the bar face down, using the Western roll. After landing pits improved (from sawdust and wood chips to a large foam rubber pad) in the early 1960s, Dick Fosbury revolutionized the event by going over the bar face up (a technique now known as the Fosbury flop). A fit organization expects that today's standard will be supplanted with a new and better standard tomorrow.

Notice, too, that the notion of a correct way to perform a task doesn't just apply to repetitive, mechanical operations such as tightening screws or cutting sheet metal. TWI is predicated on the central principle that there's a right way to do *everything*, including abstract and creative work like teaching, communicating, analyzing, and improving. When you accept this central tenet of TWI, you realize that the way TWI increases organizational fitness is nearly identical to the way that a skilled personal trainer increases physical fitness. A good personal trainer manages her clients effectively by keeping them engaged and motivated; breaks down exercises into their component parts and teaches them to her clients; adapts a client's fitness program to improve results; and knows how to keep her clients from overtraining or getting hurt.

Standard Work Versus "Scientific Management"

Talking about the correct or best way to do a task raises the uncomfortable specter of Frederick Taylor and "scientific management." In the late 1890s and early 1900s, Taylor espoused the belief that work processes could be broken down and analyzed in order to improve productivity and efficiency. In this

(continued)

regard, Taylor was ahead of his time. However, the singular image of Taylorism is a well-dressed, educated man holding a stopwatch, timing the movements of uneducated, hourly workers in overalls doing unskilled labor, and telling them what to do and how to do it.

TWI's approach to "standard work" differs dramatically from Taylor's approach. In TWI, the people actually doing the work define the best way to do it—not an external consultant or a vice president three levels removed. In a fit organization, leaders don't mandate how work should be done. Rather, they act as coaches if there are problems in following the standards, or they use their power at the top of the hierarchy to eliminate obstacles to doing the work the right way. (Paul Akers, president of FastCap, whom I wrote about in Chapter 1 and Chapter 6, is a model of this kind of leadership.) But ultimately, it's the people doing the work who are the experts, and it's they who determine the best way to do the job. Dick Fosbury is a perfect example.

How do they create the standard? In a manufacturing environment, there are three elements they consider: the pace at which they have to work in order to meet customer demand; the sequence of processes involved in producing the product; and the inventory of parts they need to do the job. In an office environment, the parts inventory isn't relevant, and the sequence of processes may apply only in some instances. Nevertheless, at its most fundamental level, the people doing the work define the simplest, easiest, most intuitive possible process to produce quality work.

Documenting and codifying best practices enables companies to become true "learning organizations." This standard work is the basis for all improvement. Done correctly, it captures the collective experience and knowledge of all the people who have worked, and who currently work, in the organization. Each person contributes to the body of knowledge and lays the foundation for future improvement. Without these standards, there can be no continuous improvement—it's impossible to perform thorough, scientific problem solving when there's no consistency in the way the work is currently done. How do you know which variables are responsible for errors if the way the work is being done varies from person to person, from day to day, from business unit to business unit? And how do you know which variables contribute to better-than-expected outcomes if there's no consistency?

Amazon provides a wonderful example of how standard work enables improvement. One of the jobs in a fulfillment center is a "stow line." Workers have a trolley full of products and a scanner. The job is to stow the products on the shelves and scan each item and the corresponding shelf number. The standard work productivity target was 20 minutes per trolley, but it often took much longer due to the scanner's battery running down. Knowing the gap between the standard and the actual performance led to a structured problem-solving session:

> How many scans could be completed during the life of the scanner battery? Did we have a process to check and reload the scanner batteries? Frontline managers didn't have any of that information, so there were several hours of low productivity at the end of every scanner's battery charge. That root-cause analysis helped us put a whole process in place to load and monitor our scanners. Now workers will never miss productivity targets because their scanner batteries are low.[5]

Even without following the letter of the TWI law, fit companies embrace the spirit of TWI: they make a habit of defining, documenting, and teaching the best way to perform the innumerable activities in the thousands of processes that operate in any organization. This best way is enshrined as the standard work. Take, for example, the customer service department at NFI Industries in Chino, California. NFI is a logistics, transportation, and distribution company with 70 warehouses across the country. Even if you know nothing about this industry, it's not hard to imagine that coordinating logistics among trucks, trains, warehouses, and distribution centers is challenging because of the incredible number of parts in motion at any one time. All you need is a flat tire on one truck, and the entire schedule for inventory replenishment at a major retailer might be disrupted.

In the past, NFI managers created standard operating procedures (SOPs) for the various processes throughout the company. The corporate SOPs were carefully collated, three-hole punched, filed, and, like SOPs in most companies . . . promptly forgotten. (That's what often happens when management creates policies and procedures and foists them upon the people who are actually doing the work. No matter how well intentioned, they become museum artifacts.)

In 2012, the company changed its approach: as Ted Makros, director of operations, explains it,

> We gave the frontline staff responsibility for identifying problematic situations, figuring out how to deal with them, documenting those approaches, and training coworkers on the improved processes. It was up to each team to determine when their new approach should become the new standard, and when it did, they typed it up and laminated it. And since it was obvious that SOPs sitting in a binder weren't helping anyone, we also requested that the procedures be visible and accessible to everyone.

The customer service SOPs are a terrific example of what happened—Figure 4.1 shows the standard work wall.

FIGURE 4.1 Standard work wall at NFI.

Actually, the customer service team doesn't call them SOPs. They call them "cheat sheets," and they like to have fun with them. Figures 4.2 through 4.4 show close-ups of several.

FIGURE 4.2 SOP for a recall item.

FIGURE 4.3 SOP for keying in a shipment.

Improving efficiency and quality of processes is important, but it's only part of the benefit to the company. Creating standard work also generates shared knowledge within each department. Rather than relying on tribal knowledge ("Ask Keiko—she's been here forever and knows how to get it done."), the communication and cooperation among all members of the group ensure that all learning is disseminated widely. That sharing of knowledge makes the company more resilient and flexible.

It's also worth mentioning that codifying standard work doesn't guarantee that it will be done properly, any more than a holding a notecard saying "Don't let your knees go past your toes!" ensures that your form while doing squats will be correct. At NFI, managers realize that training and practice are critical to embedding standard work. Moreover, when people do deviate from the standard, they reassess the cheat sheet: they examine why the person didn't follow the standard, and if appropriate, they change it. In this way, standard work becomes a living, vibrant document that's continually examined and adapted to changing situations, rather than a dusty manuscript hermetically sealed under glass.

FIGURE 4.4 SOP for receiving a pallet.

THE BEST WAY TO MANAGE

Notwithstanding the amazing record of success of TWI—remember, B-29s built by women who just left the apple pie on the windowsill—it's easy to dismiss the idea of a best way of working as something that's applicable only to the assembly line or manual labor. There's a temptation to think that a manager's (to say nothing of a higher-level leader's) job is too complex to define best practices, that the issues he grapples with are so fluid and so diverse that the job necessitates constant improvisation and adaptation. There can't be best practices for a leader.

That's flat-out wrong.

Bob Emiliani, professor at Central Connecticut State University and author of numerous articles and books on leadership, writes:

> The cause of variation in leaders' workdays often can be traced to inconsistencies in decision making and incorrect decisions which introduce errors and other forms of variability. Since much of an executive's work is decision making, a type of knowledge work, decision-making processes that lack standards can be inefficient and costly. Thus, top leaders may inadvertently create much of the variation that they encounter.[6]

It's true that best practices for a leader don't look like the detailed job instructions for someone working the fryer at McDonald's. But building—and leading—a fit organization requires the creation and deployment of *leader* standard work at all levels of the company. Just as an individual will struggle to stay healthy and reach the target level of fitness without following these best practices, so too will an organization fail to attain excellence without the executives leading the right way.

Let's take a simple example: checklists. Properly designed, they ensure that individual steps within a complicated process are both remembered completely and done correctly. NASA astronauts and ground operations use checklists for all space missions. Since the crash in 1935 of a prototype B-17 bomber, pilots use checklists when taking off and landing planes—those processes are just too complicated, and the downside risk is too great, to rely upon mere memory. The astounding safety record of both military and civilian aviation since that time is testament to the power of checklists in managing complex environments.

Checklists are increasingly finding their way into medicine as well, dramatically reducing infection and mortality rates where they're being used. Dr. Peter Pronovost has been leading the way in this area, as Atul Gawande reported in the *New Yorker*:

> The checklists provided two main benefits, Pronovost observed. First, they helped with memory recall, especially with mundane matters that are easily overlooked in patients undergoing more drastic events. (When you're worrying about what treatment to give a woman who won't stop seizing, it's hard to remember to make sure that the head of her bed is in the right position.) A second effect was to make explicit the minimum, expected steps in complex processes.[7]

But what about at the managerial level? Can leaders really benefit from the use of a tool as standardized as checklists? Business school professors and authors Chip and Dan Heath think so. They wrote about the benefits of using checklists in intricate business processes:

> Even when there is no ironclad right way [to do a specific task], checklists can help people avoid blind spots in complex environments. Has your business ever made a big mistake because it failed to consider all the right information? Cisco Systems, renowned for its savvy in buying and absorbing complementary companies, uses a checklist to analyze potential acquisitions. Will the company's key engineers be willing to relocate? Will it be able to sell additional services to its customer base? What's the plan for migrating customer support? As a smart business-development person, you'd probably remember to investigate 80% of these critical issues. But it would be inadvisable to remember the other 20% *after* the close of a $100 million acquisition. (Whoops, the hotshot engineers won't leave the snow in Boulder.) Checklists are insurance against overconfidence.[8]

One of the most common complaints about the obligation to adhere to standard work or checklists is that it limits creativity and eliminates the role of judgment and experience. Nothing could be further from the truth. In fact, they spur creativity by removing the cognitive burden imposed by attending to mundane issues. For example, a friend of mine is a painter (canvases, not houses). He arranges the colors on his palette in the same order every time he paints because when he's in the middle of creating something new, the last thing he wants is to have to search for the yellow paint. Similarly, physicians have standard questions they follow when performing a new patient intake. They ask the same questions, in the same sequence, every time. This practice ensures that they don't forget to ask anything important, and it gives them the mental bandwidth to really focus on the patient and listen to the answers. Checklists, as well as standard work, reduce ambiguity and uncertainty, thereby allowing faster action with less deliberation. As the nineteenth-century American psychologist William James might have put it, they act like well-established habits in freeing the "higher powers of mind" for creative thought.

James Hereford, COO of Stanford Health Care, has taken the simple checklist and turned it into a comprehensive management tool—and it hasn't constrained his ability to fulfill his broad responsibilities. In keeping with Emiliani's argument that leaders may inadvertently create much of the variation that they encounter, Hereford's elaborate system of "leader standard work" ensures that the *leaders'* work gets done the right way, at the right time. Beyond that, it serves to double check that the tasks people spend their time on are the tasks necessary to support the organization's strategic goals, not just the daily "administrivia" that fills so many leaders' days. He (and his entire leadership team) has created a standardized system for tracking and scheduling their activities. They've pulled their work out of their email inboxes, online calendars, and electronic documents to make it predictable and ensure that it gets done. (It also ties into the lessons of visual management, which you'll read more about Chapter 5.) Nothing gets lost; nothing gets forgotten.

Here are a few boards from Hereford's office. The board in Figure 4.5 shows his regular work during the course of a rolling four-week period. Dark gray color indicates that the task hasn't been completed; light gray color indicates that it has been done.

FIGURE 4.5 Board showing completed and incomplete work.

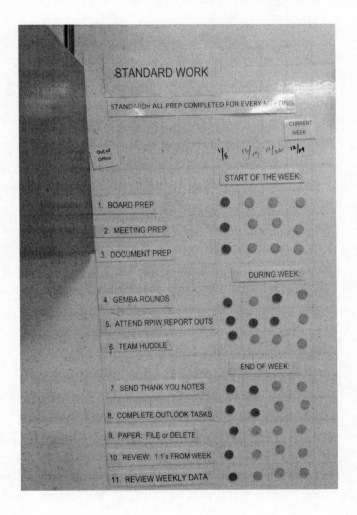

The section of his standard work board shown in Figure 4.6 shows the nonrepeating projects that are in progress and their status:

FIGURE 4.6 Standard work board showing project status.

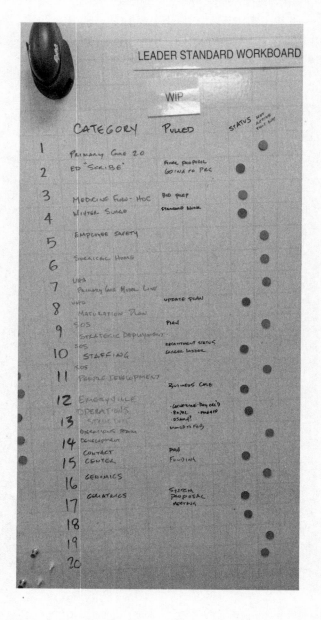

The section of the board shown in Figure 4.7 tracks his progress on answering all emails by the end of the day. The calendar at the bottom shows which departments he'll be visiting during the course of the month. The forms on the right show his annual improvement goals and the metrics for success.

FIGURE 4.7 Board showing progress in answering emails, planned department visits, improvement goals, and metrics for success.

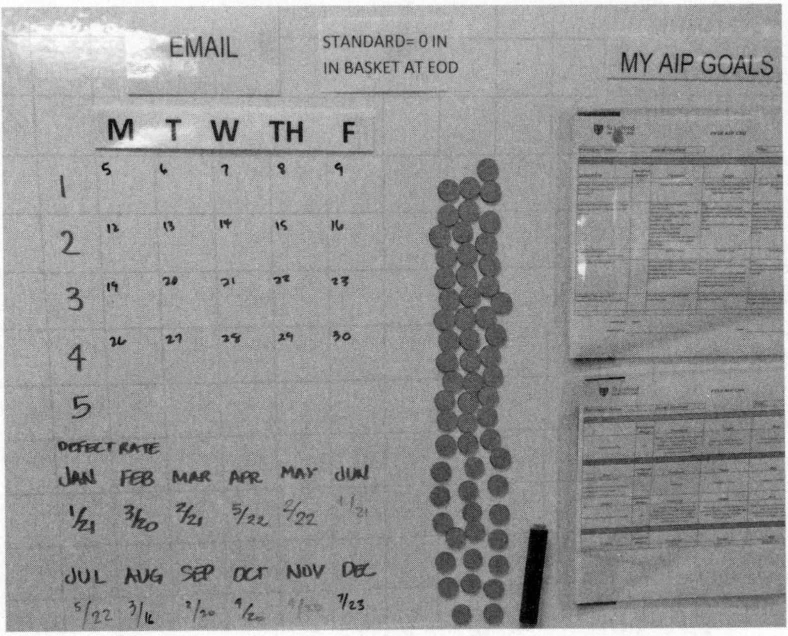

The section in Figure 4.8 shows the standard work for one of Hereford's direct reports. They review these documents at their weekly one-on-one meeting. The top section contains information on a project she's leading; the middle section shows her annual goals; the bottom document contains the weekly check of the work she's doing. The bottom document is particularly interesting, because it not only captures the work she's done in the past week, but it checks that the upcoming week's work is connected to her overall goals.

FIGURE 4.8 Standard work for a direct report: projects, annual goals, and weekly progress check.

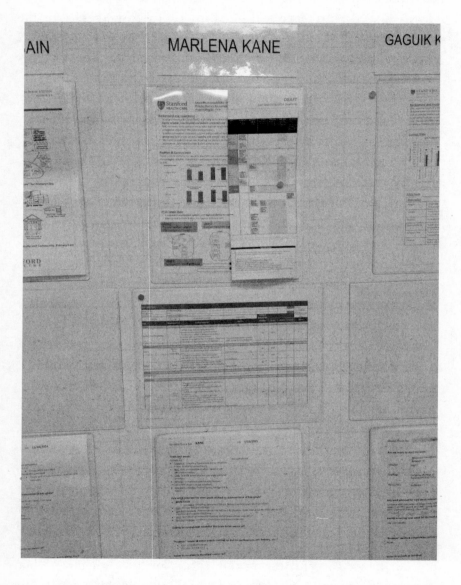

Of course, these documents tie into the standard work boards in her office so that she doesn't lose sight of the overall flow of her work, as shown in Figure 4.9.

Figure 4.9 Standard work board showing overall flow of work for a direct report.

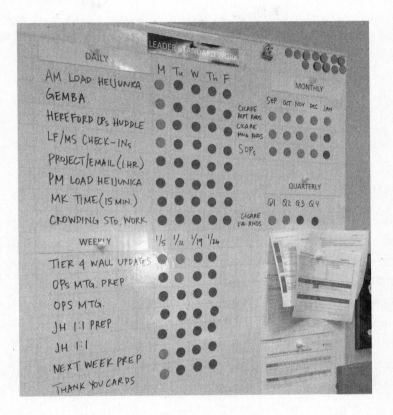

You'll note that these boards don't represent any sort of earth-shattering breakthrough in managerial theory. But in some respects, that's precisely their power: the tools help users be more efficient at running day-to-day operations, and the better they are at those quotidian activities, the more time and cognitive bandwidth they have available for strategic improvement work. Leader standard work acts as an enabler for handling the big, complex, strategic issues that any organization must deal with.

One of the most powerful, but less obvious, benefits of leader standard work is the standard calendar that everyone uses. All leaders have from 8 to 10 a.m. to prepare for patients, rather than getting pulled into meetings, roped into extraneous discussions, and so on. This two-hour block ensures that everyone has time to prepare for his or her prosaic work prior to switching focus to strategic improvement work. Moreover, this calendar enables Hereford to "tier" meetings throughout the hospital—they occur in a predictable sequence, providing a clear and rapid escalation path for all issues. Within 90 to 120 minutes, any problem can make it from the front lines to the COO for a decision or resolution.

GOING TO THE FRONT LINES

Checklists aren't a panacea for all issues, of course—many leadership issues can't be dealt with in a checklist. Nevertheless, it is possible to define and compile best practices for executives—among them, the regular presence of leadership at the front lines of the business. This makes sense: just as it's important to have a trainer regularly present at workouts, it's important to have corporate leaders regularly present where the work is being done in a company, whether that's the accounting department or the R&D lab. Going out to the trenches enables leaders to see firsthand what's happening, spot problems early, and—perhaps most important—regularly coach and train managers and supervisors in needed skills. This aspect of leader standard work enables managers to be better coaches, because it allows them to instantly see if there are any problems, including whether or not frontline workers are following their own standard work. These visits ground their improvement efforts in the actual work that's being done, not some distant perception of what's happening.

For Bryan Crowell, general manager at JD Machine Corporation, a manufacturer of precision machined components, frontline visits are woven inextricably into the fabric of his day (and all leaders' days). In addition to all the firefighting, email checking, and high-level meetings to attend, all managers are responsible for visiting their area of responsibility every day and checking on one of the seven areas deemed essential to operational excellence: quality, safety, cost, delivery, organization, employee morale, participation in the team huddle, and knowledge of daily stats and targets. There's a whiteboard that shows everyone what he or she is supposed to do and whether he or she has done it (light gray color) or not (dark gray color) (Figures 4.10 through 4.13).

FIGURE 4.10 Board showing checking of seven essential areas.

FIGURE 4.11 Close-up of board from Figure 4.10.

FIGURE 4.12 Card for quality.

FIGURE 4.13 Card for winning or losing.

As Crowell explains it, in the view of JD Machine's leadership team, just as there's a right way for a frontline worker to operate a drill press, there's a right way for managers to work, and making regular visits to the shop floor is an essential part of that best practice.

JD Machine isn't the only company that makes leader visits to the office trenches part of managerial best practices. Group Health Cooperative, a healthcare system based in Seattle with facilities around the state, does as well. The COO of the company has a standard weekly routine, spending four hours, twice per week, visiting each site. He says that it's the most important thing on his calendar, as it gives him insight into how each facility and each team is operating. It's not just his personal opinion, either. The CEO agrees that this time spent face-to-face with employees is sacrosanct: he never schedules meetings with the COO that would conflict with these visits. Both organizations consider improvement and development to be an integral part of a leader's daily work, not something that's only done when there's some free time on the calendar. The athletic parallel is clear: just as a coach or trainer is responsible for getting an athlete to higher levels of fitness, so too is the executive responsible for getting employees to higher levels of performance.

Paul Akers, the president of FastCap, is equally committed to being present at the front lines of his company. However, Akers does it as much (or more) for his own edification as for the training of his employees. In his view, the employees know how to do their work, are familiar with the problems, and know how to solve them. Going to the shop floor enables him to see those problems firsthand and then use his authority to help solve them. Akers states:

> The most important place for me is on the shop floor doing the work with my people, shoulder to shoulder. The more I do it, the better my company gets. . . . I find out the stupid work that I make my people do. I'm seeing all the things my people are struggling with that I have the power to change,

but because I don't know about it, I can't change it. The more [I do it, the more] I find out that my people appreciate it when I'm coming there to help them. To learn. To empathize. And to improve processes. . . . At the end of the day, if you want to take your company to a whole different level, get on the shop floor. Deliberately. No differently than we "3S" every day (sweep, sort, and standardize), and we have a meeting for a half hour or 45 minutes to teach and train our people for eight years that we never miss. Deliberately, in the same fashion. Get onto the shop floor on a regular basis and find out what's really happening. And I'm not talking about with your clipboard, with your iPad, with your phone taking notes—I'm talking about doing the work. Doing the work that you're requiring your people to do.[9]

For Akers, seeing and doing the work firsthand—not hearing about it in a conference room—makes him a better leader. It brings him in closer contact with the work that's being done and with the people who are doing the work. What could be more important for a leader?

Here's a critical point: these visits differ from "management by walking around" (MBWA), a concept popularized by Tom Peters and Bob Waterman in their seminal book *In Search of Excellence*. Peters and Waterman also encouraged leaders to get out of their offices and randomly walk around the company to see firsthand what's going on. However, they specifically advise managers to make their walks unpredictable, both in terms of where they go and when they go. Peters and Waterman believe that if frontline workers are expecting your visit, you won't see what's really happening on a regular basis. They argue that frontline staff will work differently; they'll clean up their work area; they'll cover up small problems. Managers and leaders won't get an accurate picture of how the processes are operating. This is a fundamentally different perspective from the one held by the leaders at JD Machine, Group Health, and FastCap—and one that, I'd argue, is antithetical to building a truly fit organization. If you've been successful in driving out fear and in destigmatizing problems, people will have no difficulty showing you the reality of their situations.

Let's go back to the fitness metaphor. Imagine that your coach only comes by unannounced to check up on you and ensure that you're following your training program. In the best case, you'd be confused (Why is my trainer at my front door at 6 a.m. while I'm still in my underwear?), and in the worst case, you'd feel disrespected (What— he doesn't trust me to do my workout?). Any momentary surge of motivation would quickly evaporate when her lack of trust in your commitment hit home. Conversely, imagine that you have regularly scheduled sessions with your coach and that you know precisely what issues you're going to address during each visit. Will that make it difficult to assess progress or diagnose problems? Probably not. In fact, it would probably make you more attentive to what you've been doing, or to the minor twinges that might indicate the onset of an injury, so that you can discuss them in full.

REVERSING THE VECTOR OF ACCOUNTABILITY

One of the most unappreciated benefits of creating and adhering to these particular managerial best practices is the powerful way in which it reverses what I call the "vector of accountability."

When people talk about accountability in an organization, typically they refer to the way in which lower-level staff is accountable to executives (or managers or supervisors) for certain actions. You can't go a week without hearing some corporate executive declaiming that workers must be held accountable if their companies are to execute and perform well. In this view, the vector of accountability always points upward, from the front lines to leadership (Figure 4.14).

FIGURE 4.14 Traditional vector of accountability: team to leader.

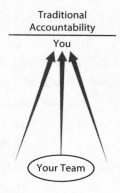

But establishing a best practice that includes visits to the trenches reverses this dynamic. When a CEO makes a commitment to visit the shop floor (or the marketing department, or the finance team, or the warehouse) each day and learn what her people are doing and what obstacles they face, she's now accountable to her team for performance. When a VP creates standard work obligating him to participate in improvement activities with his team once per month, he's making a promise that he must fulfill or risk compromising his leadership credentials. The vector of accountability flips: the leader is now accountable to the team (Figure 4.15).

FIGURE 4.15 Flipped vector: the leader is accountable to the team.

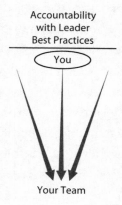

The psychological implications of this reversal are profound. All organizations comprise intricate webs of human relationships. For those relationships to be healthy and successful, there needs to be some degree of symmetry. Demanding that lower-level staff be accountable to leaders without a corresponding accountability of leaders to lower-level staff is a recipe for unhealthy, weak relationships, low morale, and disengaged employees. Indeed, according to Gallup's 2013 *State of the Global Workplace* report, 87 percent of employees worldwide are "disengaged" or "actively disengaged" at work, a stunning—and depressing—figure.[10] Reversing the vector of accountability brings balance to the interpersonal relationships in an organization, and while I'm not an industrial psychologist, it's hard to imagine that regular visits to the front lines, coupled with sincere communication, wouldn't improve this situation.

Varsity Facility Services, a national provider of janitorial services to corporations, goes one step further to make this reversal of accountability explicit. The managers' schedules are posted in the open, visible to the entire company. When a manager completes her frontline visit, her team checks the box or flips a card from dark gray to light gray to show that she did, in fact, fulfill her commitment to the team. At Varsity, it's the workers who validate the managers' completion of their standard work.

In the physical fitness environment, think how much more motivated you are when you know your trainer is showing up for your workout to provide one-to-one coaching and support. Irrespective of the actual training advice you receive, his mere presence increases your dedication to the workout program. When he commits to you to show up on time, he creates a powerful sense of mutual accountability: you'll get up 15 minutes earlier and be sure that you're out of your underwear and wearing your workout clothes when he arrives.

In the 1970s, management thinker Robert Greenleaf coined the expression "servant leadership" to describe a model of leadership in which the titular head of an organization dedicates himself to the growth and development of others who are below him on an organizational chart.[11] The managerial practice of visiting the place where work is done embodies the concept of servant leadership: the executive isn't pulling frontline employees to her walnut-paneled, carpeted office for conversations. Rather, the executive is going to the workers' territory, to learn with her own eyes and ears what's happening and to coach them in their own environment.

These examples show that managerial and leadership work is not as mysterious as you might think. While there is clearly room for variation and improvisation—and there must be, given the variability in an executive's job—there are just as clearly best practices governing how he should spend his time, with ample theory and practice to support those habits.

REDUCING PARALYSIS BY CHOICE

As a leader, you have a nearly infinite amount of flexibility in what you can work on at any given moment. Although this flexibility is rewarding and stimulating, it has a significant downside: it can lead to decision-making paralysis about *what* to do during each day.

Humans don't have an unlimited ability to make choices—after a certain number of decisions, we become mentally fatigued. A study of parole board judges in Israel showed that prisoners who appeared early in the morning received parole about 70 percent of the time, while those who appeared late in the day were paroled less than 10 percent of the time. This discrepancy had nothing to do with the merits of the cases; rather, it was due to "decision fatigue" among the judges—by the afternoon, it was easier for the judges to stick with the status quo than to invest the mental energy to carefully consider the cases on their merits.[12] President Obama has established daily habits specifically to minimize the number of inconsequential decisions he has to make in order to conserve mental energy for more important issues. Journalist Michael Lewis explained in an interview:

> The president started talking about research that showed the mere act of making a decision, however trivial it was, degraded your ability to make a subsequent decision. A lot of . . . the trivial decisions in life—what he wears, what he eats—[are] essentially made for him. He's actually aware of research that shows that the more decisions you have to make, the worse you get at making decisions. He analogizes to going shopping at Costco. If you go to Costco and you don't know what you want, you come out exhausted, because you're making all these decisions, and he wants to take those decisions out of his life. So he chucked out all his suits except his blue and grey suits so he doesn't have to think about what he's going to put on in the morning. Food is just arranged for him and he's not making any decisions about what he's eating. What most people spend most of their life deciding about, he's had those decisions removed from his life. He does this so he creates an environment, a mental environment, where he's got full energy for the decisions that are really important decisions.[13]

When you have to make many decisions—and what's the presidency but an unending series of extraordinarily difficult decisions?—you inevitably become what researchers call a cognitive miser, hoarding your mental energy. That hoarding leads to one-dimensional analysis, illogical shortcuts, and decisions that tend to favor short-term gains and delayed costs.

Bill Walsh, the legendary football coach who led the San Francisco 49ers to three Super Bowl championships in eight years, was famous for scripting the first 20 to 25 plays of each game for his team. Predetermining the early phases of the game provided multiple benefits—the ability to practice the exact sequence of plays before the game, and the ability to see how the opponent responds to certain formations—but I would argue that it had another advantage: It reduced the complexity of the game and the number of decisions that both Walsh and his quarterback faced. Scripting the first plays of the game is akin to what Columbia University social theorist Jon Elster calls "self-binding."[14] Like Ulysses lashing himself to the mast of his ship in order to prevent himself from succumbing to the Sirens' song, Walsh made the advance choice to limit his (and his quarterback's) choices and reduced the cognitive burden they had to deal with.

These two factors—the difficulty of choosing among many options, and the accumulated fatigue of decision making—are why leader standard work, and the discipline to follow it, is essential for athletic fitness or business fitness. Trainers and coaches don't give their clients multiple workout options. Even if he has a good grasp of training theory, it's too difficult for a runner, for example, to decide whether to do 8 × 400-meter repeats, or 6 × 600-meter repeats, or 4 × 800-meter repeats. The coach decides so that the athlete can focus and perform without having to waste time and energy deciding which workout is best on that particular day.

In the same way, it's too cognitively draining for an executive to continually choose which among the complex and consequential issues deserves her attention. She'll quickly get overwhelmed and default to the easiest option: checking email. Or getting a cup of coffee. Or just doing the simplest, easiest, fastest (but not necessarily most important) task. More cognitively demanding work, like coaching and mentoring her team, will fall by the wayside. That's why, like an athlete, she needs a plan, and the discipline to follow it. Of course, executives don't have coaches to determine their plans for them, so, like many of the best athletes, they're responsible for creating their own regimens.

What's your regimen?

Monday Morning To-Do List

Here are some steps that will help you create standard work.

- List the critical areas of responsibility that you need to attend to on a regular basis. This list will certainly include your direct reports (HR, finance, IT, etc.). The list should also include the major initiatives they're managing.
- List the strategic initiatives that you're responsible for and the key performance metrics that you want to track. Identify and list the drivers of those metrics. Remember that the drivers of those metrics will be deeper down in the organization.
- Determine the frequency that you need or want to check in on these people, these initiatives, and the drivers. Some will be daily, some will be weekly, and some will be monthly. Also determine how much time you need to spend with them. Fifteen minutes? Thirty minutes? One hour? Remember that coaching your team in problem solving, and not just asking for status reports, must be a regular part of these meetings.
- Create a visual system that enables you to track whether or not you've done these tasks. You can use a calendar, a board with dark gray and light gray pins, or (like James Hereford), some combination of both.
- Make sure that your standard work includes time out of your office and at the front lines with the people who are doing the daily work of the organization.
- Follow the lead of Ted Makros at NFI, and give the frontline staff responsibility for creating their own standard work. Have them identify common problems, the best approaches for dealing with them, and the way they want to document—and train people on—them. Remember that at each level of the organization, the team leader/supervisor/ manager must work together with the team to create the standard work. The creation of standard work is an integral part of the structured coaching process that develops people's capabilities.

5

Visual Management

Most office work is invisible. Sure, you can see people working at their desks, but the work itself is information residing in physical or electronic folders and inboxes. If you can't see it, you don't know whether or not the process is running well. Visual management systems provide critical information that allows you to assess the quality and pace of the work being done so that you can identify problems and make improvements—in real time, where those issues occur. They also foster teamwork and improve communications among departments that would otherwise struggle to coordinate efforts.

THE POWER OF VISUAL MANAGEMENT

Walk into any fitness center, health club, or gym in the country and you'll see yourself. Or rather, reflections of yourself. It doesn't matter whether the gym is a low-tech, Paleo diet, free weight haven one step up from a cave or a posh Park Avenue fitness emporium catering to hedge fund managers—you'll see mirrors, and lots of them. Greek myths aside, the mirrors aren't a manifestation of the customers' narcissism (although they are useful for checking out the handsome guy or the cute girl working out near you). They're actually there for an important purpose: to help people do their exercises properly. The mirrors act as a real-time check on your activity, enabling you to immediately adjust to ensure your safety and the quality of your exercise. Without immediate visual feedback, it would be terribly easy to injure yourself with poor technique. If you're getting ready to do squats with 100 pounds on your shoulders, your knees will be eternally grateful that your body is in proper alignment before you go too far down.

Visual feedback goes further than simply mirrors, of course. A golfer who can't afford to hire her own swing coach might use a video that shows her swing in slow motion, enabling her to correct errors in the process of drawing back the club head, rotating the hips, bringing the club back down, and whacking the ball. A swimmer examines videos of his stroke so that he can better understand the subtle technique improvements in the process of bringing his arms down into the water and pulling back to propel himself down the pool faster. High jumpers, pole vaulters, and athletes in other technical track and field disciplines all use video as well to improve the process by which they run, jump, and throw themselves or their implements into the air.

Today's high-tech fitness trackers—Fitbit, Jawbone, Nike Fuel-Band, and the Apple Watch, not to mention the many sophisticated cycling and running computers—take visual management to another level. They provide real-time feedback on pace, calories burned, power generated, elevation gain, and probably, in the near future, your horoscope. They provide quantitative measurements on a stunning array of factors. No matter what your fitness activity, you can get visible, quantifiable feedback on what you're doing and how well you're doing it *while you're doing it.*

By contrast, consider the typical office environment. What do you see? Mostly, it's people hunched over their computers, typing furiously. Or people hunched over their iPhones in meetings, typing furiously (but covertly). How can those workers determine whether or not they're doing their work properly? Equally important, how can you, as a leader, determine whether or not they're doing their jobs properly? And how can you know whether or not the overarching process—preparing marketing materials, or opening up new accounts, or onboarding a new employee—is functioning as well as it could? To be sure, assessing the quality of work in a modern office is more difficult than in a gym. White-collar workers generally manipulate bits and bytes of data, not kilograms of iron. Office work is, in our electronic age, largely intangible and mostly invisible. But when you can visibly track the work in your organization while it's underway, you can ensure that standard work is being followed; that the work being done is focused on the customer and not the department silo; and that the improvement mindset is reinforced by reviewing and analyzing the scoreboard every day.

The invisibility of most office work creates real problems. At best, it means that tracking the work requires weekly status update meetings with the whole team gathered in the conference room (and half the team covertly checking email.) At worst, it means that there's no way to make improvements until after the monthly or quarterly business results are in. That delay can be financially disastrous and can threaten the organization's viability. To return to the fitness metaphor, there's no way to make improvements to the process until after you've blown out your knee or overtrained and died at mile 11 in your big marathon. That's not a very good way to run a business. By the time you know that a process isn't working very well, you're facing an investment call with analysts, or you're getting pilloried on Facebook by angry customers, or lawyers are gearing up for a class-action lawsuit.

Frankly, you can't afford to wait till the end of the week, the month, or the quarter to assess your quality or your performance. That time lag may have been acceptable in 1815 and 1915, but certainly not in 2015. Information flows through the markets at Internet speed. By the time you've assembled your leadership team in the executive conference room to discuss the issue and figure out how to deal with it, it's not only too late, but you also risk running into political and cultural roadblocks to resolution. Look no further than General Motors' ignition switch fiasco in 2014. Leaving aside the (rather significant) issues of malfeasance and immorality in product development and approval of the ignition switch, the complacent, politically paralyzed management team was unable to take corrective action. The Valukas report issued by the company makes this problem painfully clear. It describes the "GM Nod," "the practice of GM managers sitting in a room, nodding in agreement at steps that need to be taken, then leaving the room and doing nothing"; and the "GM Salute," in which employees sit through meetings "with their arms folded and pointing outward at others, as if to say that the responsibility lay with them, not with the employee."[1]

Think about it: athletes, trainers, and coaches don't wait to make adjustments. They act as soon as possible. Tiger Woods doesn't wait till Sunday night at the Masters to say, "Gee, I wasn't putting very well, so I guess I should've approached Amen Corner differently." No—he changes his game plan after the first day (and maybe even after the first few holes of the day). A more dramatic example can be found in professional football. The coach doesn't wait in the locker room for the score at the end of the game to determine what to do differently— that's patently ridiculous. The coach doesn't even wait till halftime to make adjustments. That's still too late. In today's game, the coaches receive photos from an assistant in a skybox *immediately after each play* so that they can better see and analyze what the opponent is doing and change their own tactics. How quickly can you make adjustments in your organization's processes? How long does it take to see that there's a problem?

THE THREE PURPOSES OF VISUAL MANAGEMENT

At the risk of unnecessarily turning something simple into business jargon, the mirrors, photos, videos, trackers, and computers (not to mention the scoreboards) that athletes and coaches use act as "visual controls," or visual management systems, that help assess performance. These controls are an essential part of becoming fit, staying healthy, and improving. Just as athletes and coaches need visual systems to get fit and improve, so too does a company.

At their core, good visual management systems enable us to distinguish between normal and abnormal conditions. To express it slightly differently, they help us identify the gap between desired and actual conditions, between where we are and where we want to be. Once we can see this gap, we can figure out how to close it. The tremendous power of the visual controls is that we can close that gap immediately, when it occurs. Fit organizations use visual controls as a signal, a trigger, to mobilize their resources to engage in root-cause problem solving through coaching and rigorous PDSA cycles in real time, at the location of the problem—not with a ream of spreadsheets examined a week later in a conference room.

Fit companies are interested in checking three essential conditions:

> *Safe vs. unsafe:* If you're in a factory pulling glazed floor tiles out of a kiln, it would be nice to know whether the tiles are cool enough to handle. A simple red light/green light on the kiln that's tied to the internal kiln temperature would convey this critical information instantly, easily, and unambiguously. Some hospitals use color-coded syringes during procedures: blue is for saline, green is for contrast dye, red is for embolic material, and yellow is for drugs designed to break up blood clots—this ensures that patients are not injected with the wrong material. Hospitals also put radiation stickers in areas where radioactive material is being used, and real-time x-ray

machines provide a running tally of radiation dose so that doctors can determine how much more time they can safely continue a procedure.

Ahead or behind: If your production target is 100 widgets per hour, or if you're a hospital trying to discharge 80 percent of the patients by 10 a.m., it's important to know whether you're on pace. An inexpensive whiteboard with the hourly production total shows where you stand in relation to the target.

Good or bad (defective): These systems show whether the work just completed meets established quality standards or whether it's defective. A simple circuit with a light into which you can fit a milled piece of metal checks that the dimensions are correct: too big, and it won't fit into the circuit; too small, and the light won't illuminate. Notice that the visual management alerts the worker that there's a problem *at that moment*, not after the product has made it all the way to final inspection.

Good visual management systems make the gap between desired and actual conditions perfectly obvious to everyone. When that gap is clear, it's easier to improve the situation. In Michael Ballé's words, with a well-designed visual control, "We see together, so we know together, so we can act together."[2]

I've specifically used manufacturing examples in order to make the value and design of visual controls obvious and easy to picture (although, sad to say, many factories don't actually utilize this kind of visible management). However, you can create them for office environments as well with a little creativity. For example, even though safety is generally not a major concern in an office, you can imagine how useful it could be to support an ergonomic initiative reducing back pain or carpal tunnel syndrome. You could have markings on the chair or desk indicating the appropriate angle for the elbow or wrist when typing or a drawing of proper posture in a chair.

A more dramatic example of how visual management systems can improve safety comes from the Kaiser Permanente Health System MedRite program. Each year in the United States, over 1.5 million people are harmed by medication errors. The regular interruption of nurses when they're administering medications is one of the major causes of these errors. Kaiser's MedRite program, introduced in 2009, was created to reduce interruptions during medication administration. There are two key visual elements to the program (Figure 5.1):

- *No-interruption wear*: a sash or vest that signals no one should interrupt or even talk to the nurse, unless there's an emergency.
- *The sacred zone*: a space marked out on the floor with tape in front of the area where the nurse pulls and prepares medications. No one should cross or talk to a nurse who is in the zone.

FIGURE 5.1A No-interruption sash.

FIGURE 5.1B "Sacred zone" marked out in tape.

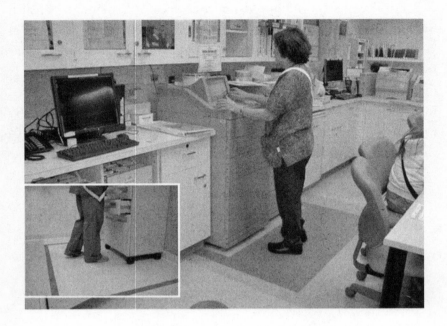

The result of these efforts has been a 50-percent reduction in the number of staff interruptions while administering medications; 15-percent faster medication passes; and an 18-percent increase in the timeliness of medication passes. Other hospitals have adopted these visual controls and seen equivalent improvements—and most important, reductions in medication administration errors.

VISUAL MANAGEMENT IN THE OFFICE

Visual controls for production pace and quality actually transfer very well to the office. Take, for instance, the visual control in an invoice-processing department shown in Figure 5.2.

FIGURE 5.2 Visual control in an invoice-processing department.

Work broken down
into two-hour
"buckets,"
by person

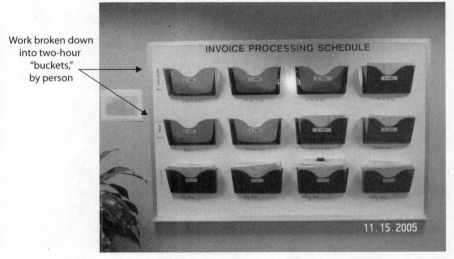

Source: Drew Locher

The top two rows belong to the two people in the department. Each plastic bucket holds two hours' worth of work. By the end of each two-hour block, the appropriate folder should be empty. The bottom row shows the backlog for each week in the month. This visual management system elegantly displays whether or not the two people in the invoice-processing team are on pace during the course of the day, and it also shows how well the process is keeping up with demand. (In this case, not so well.) If one of the plastic buckets still contains items after the two-hour time block, or if the backlog buckets aren't going down, the manager has a clear signal that there's a problem and help is needed. This example meets one of the primary needs of a good visual management system: it makes the problem obvious to everyone in real time—not at the end of the day—and allows the supervisor or manager to attack the problem quickly.

The photo in Figure 5.3 demonstrates an integrated system in which the visual control creates a cadence for office production and builds in quality checks.

FIGURE 5.3 Integrated visual control system.

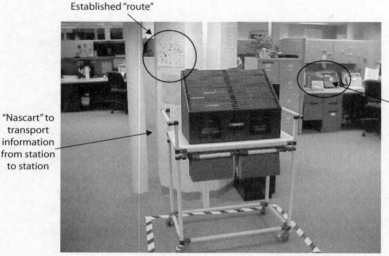

Problems are identified and action taken, if necessary, every two hours

Source: Drew Locher

This visual control (coincidentally) also operates in a two-hour time frame. Documents are picked up and dropped off to the people in the team on a set schedule, which ensures a level flow of work. Problems or errors can be identified during that pickup/drop-off round, meaning that they can't fester unnoticed for days or weeks until they're addressed.

Visual controls also provide flexible methods for ensuring quality in an office environment. For example, a software company (or the IT department of virtually any company, for that matter) could set up a light that flashes whenever new code crashes—a clear signal that there's an error needing attention. Similarly, the purchasing department of a company could use a simple paper template to ensure that forms submitted by vendors have all the data entered correctly. (Even better:

the vendors can use those forms themselves to check the quality of the information before they send it back to the company.)

SEEING THE FLOW OF WORK

If you think that visual controls are only for office grunt work, think again. A San Francisco–based boutique patent firm specializing in the medical device, clean technology, and software industries uses a simple—but very clever—visual system to manage the flow of work among its six attorneys. The corkboard shown in Figure 5.4 is in full view in their open office.

> *Extreme left-hand box.* Each tag in this box belongs to one of the attorneys. These act as horizontal "swim lanes" for allocation of work.
>
> *Middle (large) box.* The tags in this box represent the client work that will be done during the next two-week period. Each tag breaks down the specific work for each attorney and each client.

FIGURE 5.4 Visual control in a law firm.

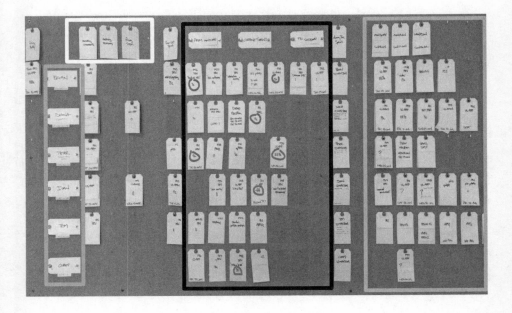

Small circles in large middle box. The numbers in these circles (on the tags in the middle box) display the estimated number of days each task will take. This keeps the lawyers from being overloaded during the upcoming two weeks and ensures that they can meet delivery dates. When the work is complete, the attorneys note the actual number of days that it took. *White-outlined box.* The three tags in this box form columns for tasks in critical stages: "awaiting comments"; "making revisions"; "filing soon." As work is completed, the attorneys move the tags from the central area in the middle box to the area below this box. This section of the board maintains the velocity of work—their production pace—by preventing client matters from falling out of sight due to other work. *Extreme right-hand box.* The tags in this box show tasks that need to be done beyond the upcoming two weeks. At the appropriate time, these tags are moved into the central section of the board in the middle box.

The movement of tags around the board shows the progress of each person's work—and more important, shows if someone is struggling and falling behind. For HR purposes, too, this visual system is beneficial. Even for the same type of task, the estimated number of days for completion differs depending on how experienced the person handling the task is. This means that work can be allocated appropriately; that salaries can be set relative to the person's abilities; and that those salaries can be adjusted when it's clear that the attorney has become skillful enough to complete standard tasks in less time.

Notice how these visual controls function the same way that mirrors or cycling computers work for the athlete. They provide clear feedback on how the overall process is functioning so that adjustments can be made to improve the performance of the system. Equally important, they give each attorney feedback on how he's doing relative to expectations—is he completing his work within the forecasted time frame, or is he falling behind? At the end of each day, both the attorney and the managing partner can see where he stands and respond accordingly.

Now, you can argue that it's easy for this law firm to make its work visible because the attorneys are doing nothing more than a fancy version of stamping out widgets: they do one type of work (patent law), which makes many of their tasks repetitive. That's true. But it's also true that your work—whatever it is—has plenty of repetitive elements. Product development? Writing product briefs, sourcing new fabrics, creating spec packages for the first sample—that's all repetitive, too. Hiring and onboarding new employees? Background checks, drug tests, getting IT network access, benefits enrollment, and so on are all repetitive. Show me a job, and I'll show you repetitive and predictable work. Not all of it, to be sure. But plenty of it, all of which can be made visible.

The jobs of executives, too, have repetitive and predictable work that can usefully be made visual. The office of James Hereford, the COO of Stanford Health Care, is a virtual shrine to visual management systems. I showed you his standard work in Chapter 4, but you may not have gotten a clear sense of just how visible he makes all of his work. The walls of his office are covered in whiteboard wallpaper, and the essential information he manages is visible in charts, graphs, and tables, with highlighted areas having boxed and circled magnets for status all around his office. Hereford pulls a lot of freight as COO, and making his work visible is critical for him to keep up with his responsibilities. Figure 5.5 shows two of the walls in his office.

FIGURE 5.5 Comprehensive visual management system.

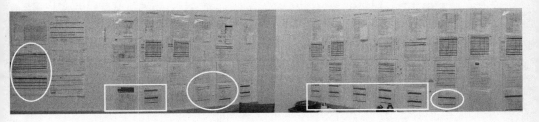

The sheets of paper on his office walls provide him with an incredible variety of information. His own personal work is up there, as are sheets representing the key projects his team is working on and the major metrics that he's tracking. At a glance he can see whether he's on top of his work (circled) or falling behind (boxed); he can see the status of the ongoing major improvement projects without having to find the information needle in the haystack of his email inbox; and he can evaluate the progress the hospital is making on the key metrics (patient satisfaction, safety, and so on) that determine his bonus.

CREATING TEAMWORK

A creatively designed visual management system has the ability to foster teamwork and cooperation among departments that typically don't work well together. Take the example of Vaisala Group, a Finnish company that manufactures environment and industrial measurement devices. Several years ago, Jorrit de Groot, the head of business development, created a comprehensive system to improve the productivity of the central R&D group and its coordination with the company's 10 business units.

Historically, the R&D group was funded with a flat percentage of overall sales. That money funded the necessary ongoing "maintenance" work in product management and engineering, along with work on advanced projects. Unfortunately, these advanced projects didn't always connect well with the future needs of the business units. And the business units, for their part, demanded as many projects as possible in order to maximize the return on "their" money—the money that their business units contributed to the general R&D budget. As a result, the R&D group had about 300 projects under way at any given time, with some people working on up to 10 projects at a time. Real progress on most of these projects was nearly impossible: the average project took four years for completion.

De Groot's multistep visual management system was a tour de force of creativity. The R&D group translated its project proposals into money—and then asked the business unit leaders to fund each initiative. The group put all the projects, along with the required ongoing maintenance, on a set of whiteboards, with estimates of how much each one would cost, in 10,000-Euro increments (based on the monthly salary expense of a full-time employee working on that project).

Each business unit received "money" that it could allocate to each project, based on the unit's own needs. The money was color-coded for each business unit and printed on paper affixed to magnets, which could be placed on the whiteboard on top of the gray estimates from R&D.

Each unit could have as much money as it wanted—but the manager understood that the money was coming out of her P&L.

Then, the business unit managers decided which projects to fund with their "money" by putting their magnets on the board provided by the R&D group. Their funding reflected the relative value of each project to their group. And they could coordinate with other business units to provide extra support for an important project so it could be completed more quickly. Conceptually, the board looked like Figure 5.6.

In actuality, the board was much messier (Figure 5.7).

The messiness of the board reflects precisely what the R&D group wanted: ongoing discussion, communication, prioritization, and negotiation between the business units and the R&D team as to which projects were truly important for the company. Even better, the boards led the business units to coordinate and cooperate: if there was a project that was valuable to three units, for example, they could pool their money to accelerate development. Or a business unit could choose to abandon a project that wouldn't be completed in a reasonable time frame because of limited funding.

FIGURE 5.6 Conceptual project funding board.

Area name <small>Contact info</small>	2011				2012				2013			
	Q1	Q2	Q3	Q4	Q1	Q2	Q3	Q4	Q1	Q2	Q3	Q4
Project 1												
Project 2												
Project 3												
Project mgmt												
Enginee-ring												

FIGURE 5.7 Actual project funding board.

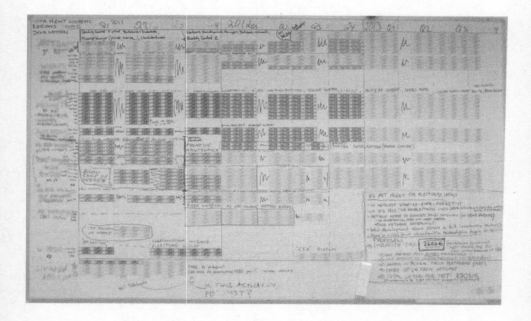

This visible (and tangible) system that de Groot designed brought the R&D group into closer contact with its "customers"; created clear priorities and eliminated half-funded initiatives; reduced the number of simultaneous projects the group was working on; and increased transparency and trust. On the business unit side as well, this system led to different behaviors and choices. Compared to an abstract number in a spreadsheet, the magnets felt more like real money, leading managers to make more rational choices in how they spent it. The system also increased the feeling of ownership for R&D projects among the business units, causing them to become much more involved in the steering of each project.

The measurable results were equally dramatic. The R&D team now averages 30 projects at a time (down from 300), with a development time frame of one year (down from four years)—all while doubling the number of product releases.

An Antidote to Sclerotic Inboxes and Flabby Meetings

If the lifeblood of the human body is, well, blood, I would argue that the lifeblood of an organization is information. It needs to flow smoothly and quickly. When it doesn't, the results can be catastrophic. Deals fail. Patients die. Spaceships blow up.[3]

Another organizational benefit of visual systems is the improvement in overall information flow. In most companies, information flow is hampered by sclerotic inboxes and flabby meetings. Valuable information gets trapped in inboxes filled with low-value status update emails. Valuable time for analysis and decision making is squeezed out of meetings in favor of tedious status update presentations that consume up to a third or even half of the meeting hour. (And let's not even talk about the time spent writing those emails and preparing the PowerPoint slides.)

Visual management systems reduce the need for those updates because the important status issues and measurements are always on display, available at any time, for anyone who's interested. It's easier (and faster) for a physical trainer to *show* you what you're doing wrong, rather than writing a doctoral dissertation on the biomechanics of the kinetic chain underlying a well-executed box jump. Similarly, visual tools reduce email and meeting burden by *showing* what's happening in a process rather than telling what's happening.

The ThedaCare Center for Healthcare Value is a nonprofit dedicated to helping healthcare organizations improve their processes. To that end, they conduct training both at their offices in Appleton, Wisconsin, and at the sites of their member hospitals. As you can imagine, coordinating those events is a laborious process—there are a lot of details that have to be addressed to make sure the events go smoothly. The visual board the organization uses to manage its "home games"—the training events at its office in Appleton—is shown in Figure 5.8.

The tasks for each event are listed down the left, while the name of each event (and date, if it's been finalized) runs across the top. The date by which each task needs to be completed is listed in the appropriate square. Once the task is done, it's replaced with a gray dot. If there's a problem, it gets a black dot.

This board isn't any sort of technological or design breakthrough in visual tools—it's not going to win a place in the Museum of Modern Art—but consider how elegantly it communicates the two critical pieces of information that anyone needs to know: when the work is supposed to be done and whether or not it's complete. No need to review the status of these events during a meeting; no need to send out lengthy emails about where things stand. If there is a problem, it's immediately visible (unlike NASA's $327 million email described in endnote 3), and people can spend their time and attention figuring out how to resolve it.

Any athlete, anyone pursuing fitness, and any coach relies upon visual systems to assess performance and chart a course for improvement.

Just like an athlete, a fit company finds ways to make its processes visible so that it can assess safety, velocity, and quality—and then align people around the commonly understood goals to make the necessary adjustments, in real time, and move to a higher level of performance.

FIGURE 5.8 Task board for hosted training events.

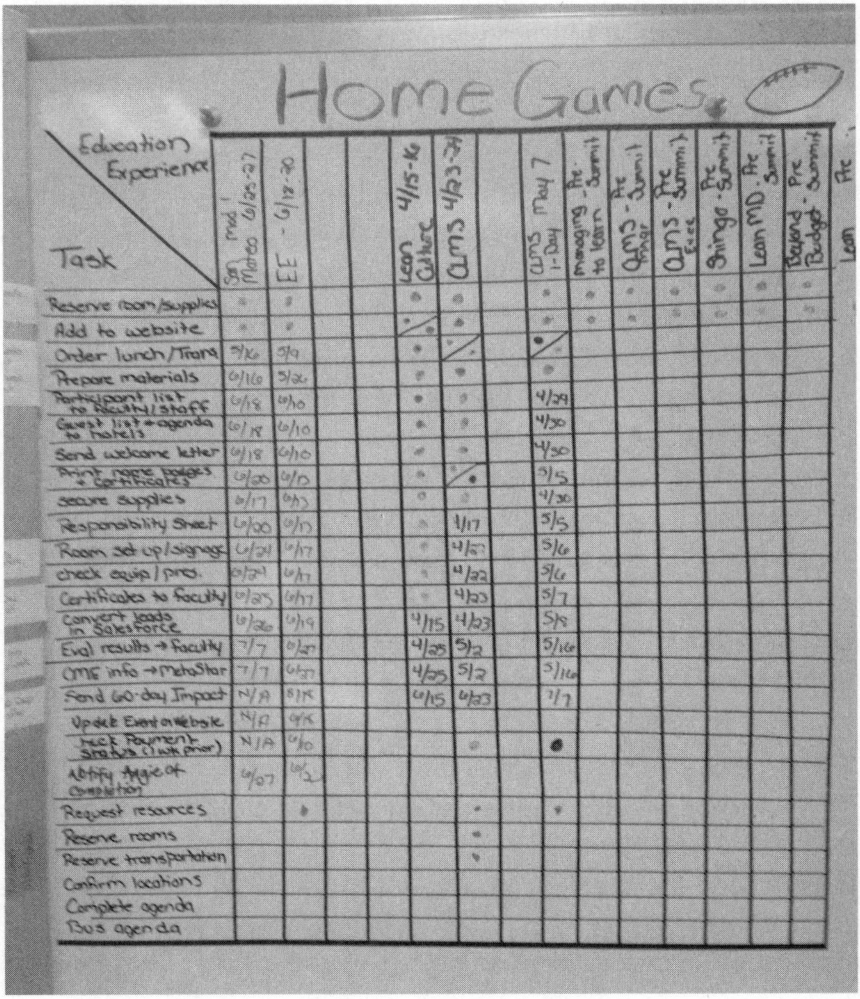

MONDAY MORNING TO-DO LIST

Here are some questions that will help you design visual management systems.

- What key performance indicators should your visual management system track? Are you creating these as a group? Are they fully understood? Who fills in the numbers? How often are they reviewed, analyzed, and acted upon?
- What safety issues do you need to make visible? Heat? Sharpness? Electricity? What kind of signal can you create to make that danger visible? For example, a bell connected to a thermometer can indicate temperature; a red light can indicate whether or not something has current running through it; a tape line on a wall can indicate the maximum safe height to stack boxes, and so on. (For more information on visual tools in a factory setting in particular, see Gwendolyn Galsworth's excellent book *Visual Systems*.)
- If you have a regular, predictable demand for your work, at what pace do you need to produce? For example, if you have a daily average of 50 invoices in A/P, you'll need to process about seven invoices per hour. Create a tally sheet for production pace, or post the numbers on a whiteboard.
- If your work is nontransactional or unpredictable (for example, product development or creation of an ad campaign), what are the major and minor milestones throughout the process? Calendarize those milestones on a whiteboard or a large sheet of paper on the wall.
- How can you measure the quality of the work being done in the intermediate and final stages? How can workers see—or show—whether their work is meeting quality standards? For example, can you have a correct sample or template available? Can you create a test that each person can run on the work when his or her portion is complete?

■ What stages or steps does the work pass through? How do you show where the work is and whether it's been through the previous step? For example, a whiteboard with Post-it Notes can show where each project sits in the pipeline.

■ How can you enable people to signal that they need help because they're falling behind or because they don't know how to do something?

6

The Coaching Triangle

*B*uilding a fit company requires leadership to invest significant chunks *of their time and creativity in the development of their employees. When you coach properly, you're engaging a person in meta-work—in thinking about how his or her work is done, and how to do it better. Good coaching doesn't just result in improved performance; more important, it enables people to improve the way the work itself is done. Done properly, the process of coaching employees develops their analytical acuity and problem-solving skills. The ultimate goal of coaching and development is the creation of an organization filled with scientific thinkers, fluent in the Plan-Do-Study-Adjust approach to improvement. To get there, you'll need to follow the three principles of the Coaching Triangle: participate; go and see; and show respect.*

If you ever want to find James Hereford, the COO of Stanford Health Care, you don't need to ask his assistant. His office is papered in whiteboard wallpaper, and in a place of honor, you'll find a chart (Figure 6.1), updated each month.

FIGURE 6.1 Coaching schedule.

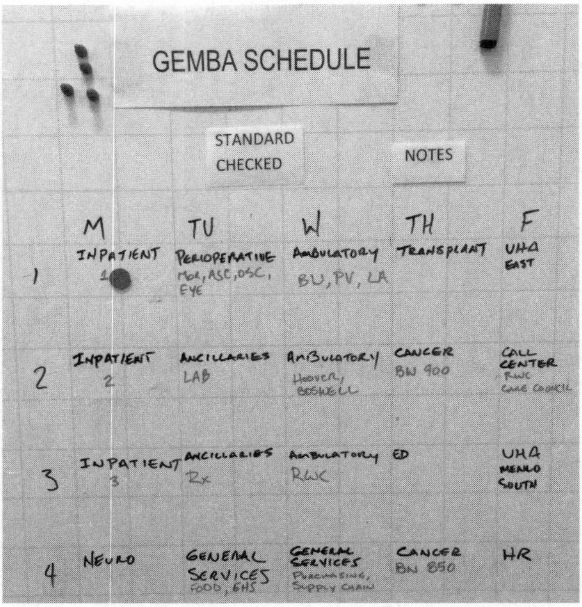

This is his coaching schedule. He visits a different department each day to observe and learn firsthand what's happening; to help solve problems; and to engage the leaders in those departments in structured development. He does this every day, without fail, because in an organization as large and complex as Stanford Health Care, the only way to ensure not just excellence but continued improvement is to rigorously devote time and attention to coaching.

Coaches are essential to achieving athletic excellence. Professional sports teams all have multiple coaches, to say nothing of an army of assistant coaches, trainers, and nutritionists tending to the athletes on the team. The same is true in individual sports: there's not a single top-ranked golfer or tennis player who doesn't have an entourage whose sole purpose is to elevate the performance level of the player. Even individuals just aspiring to lose a few pounds and improve their cardiovascular fitness employ trainers to guide their workouts and keep them motivated. Good trainers design programs that address weaknesses, enhance strengths, avoid injuries, and keep the individual motivated to keep working out, even in a cold, predawn February rain.

In the business world, the leaders—executives, managers, and supervisors—must be the coaches for the organization. Creating a fit company requires those leaders to invest significant chunks of their time and creativity in the development of their employees. To be sure, that's not easy. The demands on an executive's time are formidable, particularly in a highly connected global marketplace where problems can—and do—erupt without regard to the time zone in which they work. Nevertheless, the primary responsibility of leaders is the coaching and development of their workers. In fact, it's precisely the coaching and development of workers at all levels that enables a fit organization to thrive in turbulent, complex environments. Technology regularly changes, new competitors enter markets all the time, regulations shift unpredictably—elevating employees' capabilities and level of performance is the only thing that provides the fit organization with a sustainable competitive advantage.

Here's the truth: managing *is* coaching. Leaders must go from spending 80 percent of their time in their offices to 80 percent of their time where the work happens. Your primary job as a leader/coach is to create more coaches—to boost the capacity and fitness of your employees so that they in turn can develop others. Read all the books you want about the laws of leadership, the levels of leadership, the challenges of leadership, the art of leadership; feel free to study the leadership lessons of Jesus Christ, Sun Tzu, Abraham Lincoln, and Winnie the Pooh. But the simple fact is this: if all you do is develop the capabilities of your employees, your organization will win every challenge it takes on.

The fittest leaders and the fittest companies see it this way as well. Geoff Colvin, in his book *Talent Is Overrated*, writes,

The CEOs of top-performing companies agree that people development is at the center of their jobs. Indeed, the biggest investment involved may be the time of the CEO and other executives. At McDonald's, for example, CEO Jim Skinner personally reviews the development of the company's top 200 managers. At GE, [CEO Jeff] Immelt reviews the top 600. Bill Hawkins, CEO of Medtronic, says he spends 50 percent of his time on people issues, and many other top CEOs report similar percentages—making this the largest time commitment they have. Lots of companies claim they they're interested in developing leaders, but the University of Michigan's Noel Tichy, a top authority on the subject, says testing their commitment is easy: "Just show me the CEO's calendar."

The CEO's time is only the beginning. Many of these chiefs note the "cascading" effect of what they do: As their direct reports see what the boss is focusing on, they also become devoted to developing people, as do their subordinates, and so on.[1]

In the context of physical fitness, "development" is pretty clearly understood: increased strength and flexibility, greater cardiovascular endurance, perhaps rehabilitation from an injury or some chronic pain. In the context of athletics, "development" includes all of that, plus speed, quickness, agility, and sport-specific skill improvement. But in the context of work, "development" is an ambiguous word. What does development mean? What precisely goes into employee development? What are the objective outcomes? And how do you do it? Ask 10 people, and they'll provide you with at least 11 different answers.

The Goal of Coaching

Everyone in the business world needs coaching. Not just beginners, not just people who are trying to acquire a new set of skills. Everyone, including—and in fact, especially—individuals like you who are already performing at impressive levels.

In most activities, once a person reaches a certain level of skill, his growth and learning slows or even stops. Unless he's decided to become a professional and make a living by playing golf, or surfing, or playing the violin, he'll practice just long enough to get sufficiently comfortable to enjoy it without too much frustration—and then he'll stop the "deliberate practice" that got him to that point. He's made it through the four classic stages of skill acquisition—unconscious incompetence; conscience incompetence; conscious competence; unconscious competence—and is now content to enjoy his level of accomplishment.[2] Of course, for a professional athlete who wants to dominate the sport, there is no "good enough." Michael Jordan, Tiger Woods, Serena Williams, Jackie Joyner-Kersee—these athletes never stopped trying to improve. (The 10,000 hours of practice that Malcolm Gladwell made famous in his book *Outliers* applies to people like these who don't stop when they get "good enough," but who continue to develop and refine their skills.) Even for the average person seeking to become fitter and healthier, however, there's no end to the coaching and training they need.

This model of skill acquisition and plateauing applies to the business sphere as well. Welders, account executives, surgeons, teachers—all of them begin their careers wallowing in the shallow waters of unconscious incompetence and gradually progress to the deep end of unconscious competence. But then, unless their jobs change significantly, or they take a new (and often higher) position in the organization, their growth and development stall. This doesn't mean that they can't get better at their jobs, only that they've reached a level that's good enough to fulfill their responsibilities, and fulfill them comfortably.

However, that's not good enough for a fit organization. A fit organization doesn't settle for unconscious competence. It continually seeks to develop the skills and capabilities of its people.

Just as in the athletic sphere, coaching can help people in the workplace push past their level of comfort and continue to improve. Surgeon and author Atul Gawande noticed that after eight years of operating, his performance, as measured by the number of surgery-related complications, had plateaued. As an experiment, he enlisted a retired surgeon to coach him. Over a nine-month period, the coach would join Gawande during both the preoperative planning and the actual operations, make observations, and discuss them with Gawande. His suggestions were all around small issues—how Gawande held his elbows, or where the surgical draping was positioned—but the accumulation of these subtle changes resulted in an improvement in Gawande's surgical complication rate. In short, focused coaching made Gawande a better doctor.

However, coaching doesn't only improve performance in physical/technical activities, such as hitting a golf ball or performing surgery. Coaching also improves performance in knowledge work. As Gawande explains in a *New Yorker* magazine article, researchers in California studied teacher skill development during the 1980s. They found that workshops led teachers to use new skills in the classroom only 10 percent of the time. Even when a practice session with demonstrations and personal feedback was added, fewer than 20 percent deployed the new skills. But when coaching was introduced—when a colleague watched them try the new skills in their own classroom and provided suggestions—adoption rates exceeded 90 percent. Teachers receiving coaching were more effective in the classroom, and their students did better on tests.[3] Focused coaching made them better teachers.

Coaching, essentially, engages a person in meta-work—in thinking about how their work is done and how to do it better. Good coaching results in improved outcomes—a longer javelin throw, a lower rate of surgical complications, higher student achievement—but even more important, it enables people to improve the way the work itself is done.

I know that I promised I wouldn't write about Toyota in this book. To that end, I've avoided any mention of how it deploys specific tools. However, I think it's valuable to turn to Toyota in this particular instance, because the company provides a shining example of what you should strive for as you incorporate regular, structured employee development into your organization. At Toyota, coaching between managers and frontline workers, between more experienced and less experienced people, is part of the company's DNA. It's how lessons are transmitted, how improvements are made, how changes are woven into the fabric of the way the company operates. Charles Fishman explains the result:

> What is so striking about Toyota's Georgetown factory is, in fact, that it only looks like a car factory. It's really a big brain—a kind of laboratory focused on a single mission: not how to make cars, but how to make cars better. The cars it does make—one every 27 seconds—are in a sense just a by-product of the larger mission. Better cars, sure; but really, better ways to make cars. It's not just the product, it's the process.[4]

What is employee development in the workplace? At Toyota—at a fit company—it's just this: engaging people in the examination of their own work so that they can figure out how to improve it. When it's done properly, the process of leading employees through this examination develops their analytical acuity and problem-solving skills. Remember that the ultimate goal of coaching and development is the creation of an organization filled with scientific thinkers. As I mentioned in Chapter 1, the fit organization wants all workers to be proficient in the scientific method of problem solving: Plan-Do-Study-Adjust (PDSA). PDSA thinking directs people to identify and tackle the root causes for the problems they see, rather than repeatedly—and ineffectively—putting Band-Aids on visible symptoms. The result is that, as Carolyn Brodsky of Sterling Rope says, "The most powerful improvement tool we have is our employees' brains."

Of course, many organizations have some sort of informal development program in place. Or perhaps they have a formal coaching program, but it's episodic—every month or every quarter. That's not good enough. It wouldn't be sufficient for tennis star Roger Federer to talk to his coach once a month, and it's not sufficient for you to coach your team (or for your managers to coach theirs) once a month. Fit companies are so successful because development and coaching are embedded into the daily fabric of work for both the frontline worker and the executive. The regular and predictable cadence of coaching and development brings leaders to the front lines every day, allowing for steady growth and improvement.

Structured employee coaching and development leads to better products and services, and to better processes for delivering these products and services. But the most important outcome is the development of better people. The fit leader creates employees who are better able to analyze everyday processes and invent new ones.

The Three Elements of Effective Coaching

A successful long-term coaching relationship—for a professional athlete or for an average person who just wants to get in better shape—is part alchemy and part common sense. A coach who works well with one athlete might not connect with a different athlete. Similarly, techniques that work well for one athlete may not work for another. While the alchemical element of coaching is unquantifiable, however, we can at least identify the commonsense part of a successful coaching relationship: participate, go and see, and show respect (Figure 6.2).

FIGURE 6.2 Elements of effective coaching.

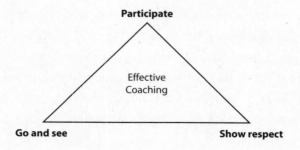

Participate

The best personal trainers and coaches don't just prescribe the workout—they model the exercises and participate in the activities they're prescribing for their clients. The great coaches are there on the court or on the field with their athletes. Obviously, due to physical limitations (or just advancing age), they may not lift the same amount of weight or do the same number of repetitions, but they participate to the extent they're able. If you've ever taken a spin class, you know that most of the time, the leader of the class rides the whole session with the group (which, in my experience at least, is a lot more motivating than having her hector me from the floor). Sixty-year-old Jim Caldwell, one of the most widely respected coaches in the National Football League, used to go over the offensive game plan each week, imitating a strong safety or a weakside linebacker to give his quarterback different looks.[5]

Similarly, great business leaders participate directly in the development of their people. They don't outsource the coaching to the HR department or to someone in the operational excellence team. They do it themselves.

The importance of this commitment is clearly expressed in a comment made by John Toussaint, the former CEO of ThedaCare, a community-owned health system. Despite eye-popping increases in the cost of medical care, Toussaint dramatically improved hospital performance during his eight-year tenure, doubling revenue and operating margin, all while receiving numerous awards for quality of patient care. When asked why other hospitals struggle to follow ThedaCare's lead, Toussaint replied:

> The biggest mistake that is made is that the senior leaders or the CEO delegates this work to somebody from a department or a [Six Sigma] Black Belt and says, "Here, you just go do lean. And then come back and report to me." This is about everyone's engagement, from the CEO to the front line nurse and everyone in between. If people aren't going to commit to being engaged at all levels of the organization, they shouldn't try this.[6]

It's worth pointing out that unlike the world of athletics or physical fitness, where a trainer or coach may not be able to do the same work as the athletes, the best business leaders engage people's hearts and minds by engaging in their own improvement work. They don't simply issue proclamations about the importance of improvement and development, and they don't just "support" what people are doing—they actively participate themselves. Art Byrne, former CEO of Wiremold, understands how essential it is for executives to participate in the development of employees and the improvement of work processes. In 10 years under his leadership, Wiremold quadrupled sales, raised gross profit from 38 percent to 51 percent, and increased the value of the company by nearly 2,500 percent. Byrne says,

> You can't just send a memo. You've got to lead it. Show them by example, do it on the shop floor. Learn by doing.

That doesn't mean that the CEO has to clean and oil the drill press or enter orders into the computer system with the customer service department every day—although once in a while, it wouldn't be a bad idea. For one thing, it's nearly impossible to coach effectively and improve the fundamentals without knowing the work itself. As Paul Akers at FastCap points out, it's also an incredibly powerful way to learn what your frontline employees deal with on a regular basis. (The disconnect between what the CEO thinks is going on and the reality of life in the organization can be shocking—just watch a few episodes of CBS's *Undercover Boss*.) However, it does mean that the leadership team must be involved in the improvements being made so that the team members know what's happening, and so that the workers can see the leadership commitment. Without that participation, leaders who preach the importance of improvement become hypocrites.

Go and See

The real work of the organization isn't done in the conference room. The real work of the organization isn't contained within monthly financial statements or elaborate internal reports. The real work is done on the shop floor, and in the product development department, and at the customer service desks. Effective coaching requires that leaders get out of their offices and "go and see" the reality of what's happening with their own eyes.

If an athlete suffers from repetitive injuries or continually fails to perform an exercise properly, the only way for the coach or trainer to diagnose the root cause is to see firsthand what the athlete is doing. Discussing the situation in the training room after the fact is inefficient at best and ineffective at worst. Similarly, in a work environment, if there are repeated order entry errors or continual problems getting your marketing materials ready on time, you have to watch the process, and the workers in the process, with your own eyes to help them improve the way work is being done. Just like Gawande's coach in the operating room, you have to be physically present to see the little details that will enable you to coach effectively.

There's another powerful benefit to "going and seeing": it helps to break down the walls of privilege that separate the rank-and-file workers from the executives. Leaders typically don't get out to the front lines very much, so when they do, employees assume that there's a major problem, or that people are about to be laid off. As an example, prior to the bankruptcy of General Motors in 2009, the company's executives kept themselves in almost total isolation from the frontline workers—they ate catered meals in a private dining room and used a special elevator that took them directly from the garage to their offices on the fourteenth floor. (I probably don't even need to mention that entrance to that floor was by invitation only.) Or consider Jill Barad, the former CEO of Mattel, who refused to ride in elevators with anyone else in the company. If one of these executives showed up in the regular offices or in the assembly plant, everyone knew the only possible reason was a major problem, and someone was going to pay.

The late Ken Iverson, who revolutionized the U.S. Steel industry at Nucor, decried these barriers of privilege as an obstacle to improvement:

> Inequality runs rampant in most business corporations. I am referring now to hierarchical inequality which legitimizes and institutionalizes the principle of "We" vs. "They." . . . The people at the top of the corporate hierarchy grant themselves privilege after privilege, flaunt those privileges before the men and women who do the real work, then wonder why employees are unmoved by management's invocations to cut costs and boost profitability. . . . When I think of the millions of dollars spent by people at the top of the management hierarchy on efforts to motivate people who are continually put down by that hierarchy, I can only shake my head in wonder.[7]

For many leaders—or at least leaders in large organizations—this separation makes "going and seeing" an emotionally fraught process. One CEO I know told me that for the first two months after he started walking around his company, workers scurried away from him in an effort to avoid any contact—a sensible response from the workers, but one that was personally hurtful for the CEO. Over time, however, his daily visits to the factory floor—his commitment to "go and see"— demonstrated his sincerity toward coaching employees and helping them improve their work.

The Ohno Circle

The Ohno Circle is a legendary teaching device created by Taiichi Ohno, the father of the Toyota Production System. He would get on his hands and knees, draw a chalk circle on the floor, tell a manager to stand inside the circle, and

(continued)

issue the simple directive, "Watch." Several hours later Ohno would return and ask what the manager had observed. Usually Ohno had noticed a problem earlier and wanted the manager to learn to spot it. If the manager didn't see anything wrong, or saw something other than what Ohno had already seen, he would tell the manager to stay in the circle and watch some more. This exercise could go on for an entire eight-hour production shift . . . and then might be repeated the next day.

As Yogi Berra (is reputed to have) said, "You can observe a lot by watching." The Ohno Circle is the apotheosis of this Yogi-ism. What better way to understand what's actually going on than by doing nothing *but* looking?

When you hear about problems in the workplace while sitting in a conference room, you can't truly see what's happening, and you can't see the context in which it takes place. Going to where the work is occurring gives you the ability to see a process in action with your own eyes and make intelligent suggestions about how to improve it. It provides you with a deep understanding of what your workers are dealing with as they do their jobs.

It's not as easy as it seems to stay focused on the activities in front of you. Your feet hurt, you get hungry, you need to go to the bathroom, your attention wanders. In a factory, you have forklifts nearly running you over. In an office environment, it's hard to see much more than people pecking away at their computers. But you can notice how often people are interrupted, or need to search for information, or have to clarify or correct information they've gotten from someone else.

(continued)

It's helpful, therefore, to keep in mind a standard list of questions to keep you focused. Some valuable questions are these:

Why is the worker doing that?
Where is the worker going? Why?
Does the worker know what to do? How do you know?
What is the worker waiting for?
If something is wrong, is it immediately apparent?
Can you see what a person is working on?
Can you tell if the process is on track?
If there are delays, are the reasons clearly visible?

Of course, the answer to any of these questions is far less important than the questions themselves. The key is to learn to ask the questions in the first place. The questions are the lever for continuous improvement—and for organizational fitness.

Show Respect

There may be some abusive coaches around these days, but by and large, the best coaches and personal trainers possess a deep and abiding respect for their players or clients. A trainer who disdains his overweight clients' physical limitations will very soon be looking for a new line of work. In the office or in the factory, a managerial bully will quickly lose the respect and support of her team (and probably wind up in the HR department facing harassment charges). Treating people with dignity and respect is unquestionably a prerequisite for effective coaching.

A fit leader, and a fit company, demonstrates respect for all of the company's people. Few companies exemplify that commitment as much as Barry-Wehmiller, a $2 billion global supplier of capital equipment, manufacturing technology, and services. The company's home page on the web doesn't boast about its world-beating products or its operational excellence or about how many customers it serves. The stories and pictures there feature employees talking about how they feel respected and valued. In fact, from the company's perspective, its products and services are simply a means to an end: "We're more than just a successful capital equipment and engineering solutions firm. We're an organization fiercely committed to improving the lives of our team members across the globe." CEO Bob Chapman expresses it this way:

> Step inside any one of our 100 locations around the globe and you'll feel it: a culture of care, compassion and human connection. Our commitment to our people-first culture runs deep and has inspired a leadership model that places a priority on improving the lives of the people who make our business possible.[8]

These are not idle words. Chapman is completely dedicated to his employees, even while fulfilling his fiduciary duties as the CEO. He tells a story of a conversation at a conference:

> Somebody from a major corporation asked me, "What return on investment are you seeing in this, Bob?"
>
> "So why would I try to calculate the return on investment of being a good steward of the lives entrusted to me?" I replied.
>
> And he said, "Well, our accountant would go nuts if you didn't do that."
>
> I said, "I never even asked my accountants about something like this. This is a fundamental belief."[9]

There are hundreds (if not thousands) of examples at Barry-Wehmiller that prove these words aren't just marketing hot air. It's worth telling one typical story so that you can see what this concern looks like:

Al was a 57-year-old machinist when he was hired as a weekend shift worker in 2010. He was laid off from his previous job when he asked for insurance coverage through his employer. (Previously he had gotten insurance through his wife's job, but she had just been laid off due to the recession.) Al was depressed, angry at the world, and withdrawn, and he was treating people badly, including his family. When he was hired, he was just happy to get a job so he could make some money, be left alone, and retire after 9 or 10 years. Al wasn't looking for anything else: he had been a machinist his whole working life, and all he wanted to do was machine parts.

Eventually, Al's manager asked him to take on the newly created role of team leader. The weekend shift has many young workers, and the site's leadership team felt that Al's experience and knowledge of machining would benefit them. Al was scared to take on the new role—he had never had that kind of responsibility before—but he finally accepted the job because he wanted to help both the site's leadership team and the younger machinists. Al was coached extensively on communication, confrontation, and effective coaching skills. He developed into a great lead and became a trusted resource for the younger workers when they needed help with both machining and other issues.

Four years later, Al is dramatically happier. He's no longer depressed, and he and treats everyone kindly and with respect. Although he never had the confidence to speak publicly even in front of a few friends, he now sits on the board of his church. The Barry-Wehmiller environment has changed Al's life completely. In Al's words: "I feel like a winner."

Now, Al's personal development is certainly a great story. However, the really remarkable thing is that Barry-Wehmiller—a multibillion-dollar international conglomerate—also knows it. And tells it. And celebrates it. That's respect for people of the highest order. As Bob Chapman says,

My proposition is that you have to start from "We actually care." And then from that environment we give them the tools to care, which means allowing them to release the human potential, not the process potential. The process is just the way we tap in to the human potential, and we celebrate the individual, not the numbers. The numbers are a by-product.[10]

It's worth emphasizing that Al's growth as an employee and as a leader depended on respectful coaching. Respect is essential to the coaching relationship because the cognitive cost of disrespect is so high. Indeed, rudeness actually impairs the ability to perform complex tasks requiring creativity, flexibility, and memory recall. One experiment at the University of Florida demonstrated that people on the receiving end of incivility generated 25 percent fewer and less creative ideas than people who weren't subjected to rude behavior. And a large-scale survey across multiple industries found that people who felt disrespected *intentionally* decreased their work effort as well as the quality of their work, while also losing work time worrying about the incident.[11]

So far, this is pretty straightforward stuff. Most people don't go into work meaning to be a bully or a condescending jerk, and it's intuitively obvious that it's hard to coach and develop someone who feels threatened or disrespected by you. However, "showing respect" doesn't simply mean that the leader is polite—although that's necessary—and it certainly doesn't require the leader to be a managerial cream puff. Showing respect includes something far subtler and more difficult to do on a regular basis. It means appreciating people's ability to learn, grow, and develop, and honoring their desire to do a good job. It means challenging people to extend themselves beyond what they think they're capable of. That kind of respect can be uncomfortable. It requires the willingness to confront people and show them that their level of performance—whether that's their current 10K time or the new process they've designed for handling mortgage applications—is good, but not good enough, and that with more effort and deeper thought they could do better. Showing respect means seeing that people have an infinite ability to grow and challenging them to do so. It means emphasizing the "continuous" part of "continuous improvement."

A coach who shows respect doesn't provide answers; rather, she asks questions that force the learner to think for herself. To be sure, it's much faster and easier to simply answer questions directly, and that's awfully appealing given the harried daily life of an executive. It also *feels* respectful—after all, she's providing polite, thoughtful, and helpful responses to genuine questions. But giving answers disrespects the learner' capacity for learning. The direct transfer of knowledge short-circuits the learning cycle, which stunts the person's development and curtails true understanding. This dynamic is beautifully described by Atul Gawande:

> [Robert Osteen] was an unusual teacher. He never quite told you what to do. As an intern, I did my first splenectomy with him. He did not draw the skin incision to be made with the sterile marking pen the way the other professors did. He just stood there, waiting. Finally, I took the pen, put the felt tip on the skin somewhere, and looked up at him to see if I could make out a glimmer of approval or disapproval. He gave me nothing. I drew a line down the patient's middle, from just below the sternum to just above the navel.
>
> "Is that really where you want it?" he said. Osteen's voice was a low, car-engine growl, tinged with the accent of his boyhood in Savannah, Georgia, and it took me a couple of years to realize that it was not his voice that scared me but his questions. He was invariably trying to get residents to think—to think like surgeons—and his questions exposed how much we had to learn.
>
> "Yes," I answered. We proceeded with the operation. Ten minutes into the case, it became obvious that I'd made the incision too small to expose the spleen. "I should have taken the incision down below the navel, huh?" He grunted in the affirmative, and we stopped to extend the incision.[12]

Showing respect typically means listening more than talking, which allows the learner to think and to experiment. It's the only way people really learn deeply.

TEACHING SCIENTIFIC THINKING

When you meet with a really good trainer or coach, your conversation isn't random. Even if the tone is casual, even if he asks how your kids, your dog, and your bridge game are doing, he doesn't allow the discussion about your training to wander aimlessly. The conversation is structured so that he can find out the critical issues affecting your training: your overall health and energy level, your motivation, whether you have any aches and pains, what you've been doing since the last time you worked together, what results you've seen in your training, and so on. Touching on these key points is part of the best practice for coaching.

Participation in improvement, making regular and predictable coaching visits to the organizational trenches to see firsthand what's happening, and showing respect for employees are part of the best practice—or, to use the language of Chapter 4, the standard work—for coaching in the workplace. But what do you say to people on the front lines when you're actually there? How do you help them through the meta-work of examining their own job processes? How do you avoid (the easy trap of) giving answers instead of asking questions? Casual conversation won't get you there. You need a structure for your coaching—and you need to practice that structure until it becomes second nature.

Remember that the goal of employee development is to instill the discipline of scientific thinking throughout the organization. As with any new skill, acquiring this discipline requires practice for the leader who wants to coach effectively. After all, coaching is itself a skill that needs to be learned through structured and coached practice, beginning with small steps. Management expert Mike Rother suggests that the coach should ask a standard series of five questions:

1. What is the target condition? (In other words, where do we want to be in terms of speed, quality, cost, safety, etc.?)
2. What is the actual condition now?
3. What obstacles are preventing you from reaching the target condition, and which one are you addressing now?
4. What is your next experiment (and what do you expect)?
5. When can we go and see what you've learned from that experiment?[13]

Notice how these questions ensure that the leader adheres to the three elements of effective coaching: the leader must participate in improvement for this conversation to occur; the leader must go and see the results; and the leader shows respect by asking questions rather than giving answers. Notice, too, how the process embeds the PDSA or scientific method in the coaching interaction by incorporating hypothesis, experiment, and evaluation into the dialogue. The results of this kind of interaction over the long term are processes that run better and employees who think better. In this approach, the learning that accumulates during the course of improvement is as important as the improvement itself. Will Blount of Ruffwear says that this process "reinforced my confidence that we have all the tools to solve our own problems; we are self-reliant and hold the keys to our destiny."

Ultimately, this coaching is integral to the development of organization-wide standard work that I describe in Chapter 4. The relentless questioning, the focus on experiments, the clarification of the gap between where we are today and where we want to be tomorrow is a structured way of identifying and defining the current best practice for any particular job. This approach toward performance improvement is fundamentally different from issuing an edict from the executive offices that "we have to do better," or worse, launching a tirade at people for not reaching organizational goals. By helping people figure out *how* "to do better," coaching leads to the creation of the standards that enable further improvement.

Obviously, coaching in this manner is time consuming. In fact, it's designed to be time consuming. Just as athletes need "deliberate practice" to master their sports, so too do leaders need deliberate practice to master coaching. Real employee development must go far beyond casual conversations about how a person's day went or encouragement to delegate more often. It requires a repeated, structured interaction that maximizes the leader's coaching effectiveness while at the same time building analytical skills in the learner. To those executives who say they're too busy with other demands on their time, I would ask them to consider the alternative—an organization filled with people who don't know how to solve problems and improve their work themselves, and who therefore continually push problems up the hierarchy for resolution. An organization like that can never move fast enough to stay competitive in today's economy.

MONDAY MORNING TO-DO LIST

Here are some ideas to begin the practice of coaching.

- Identify the people and the departments you want to coach.
- Create a list of standard topics to cover and standard questions to use in your coaching process. (Mike Rother's book *Toyota Kata* is an excellent resource for this.)
- Set up meetings with the people you'll be coaching to explain the process and address any concerns.
- Make a visible chart to hold yourself accountable for fulfilling your coaching duties. (Refer to the standard work examples in Chapter 4 for ideas on this.)
- Research coaching opportunities for yourself.

Afterword

No magic potion fueled my journey from dead-last runner in eighth grade to competitive college athlete. My progress was incremental, with setbacks due to injury, to overtraining, and to undertraining. But during the course of those nine years, I studied and learned how to train and race better. I became a student of the sport—and of my own body. By the end of my career, I was not just a better athlete, but a smarter athlete.

The organizational journey from mediocre to outstanding—from flabby to fit—is similar. You need to study the way your organizational processes function on the macro level, and how individual jobs are done on the micro level. You'll have to become a student of your own company so that you can build better processes as well as more capable people.

At this point, you may be disappointed that I haven't provided any specific tools for you to use in this journey. You might also feel that the ideas I've presented are too vague to implement quickly and easily. You're right.

That was by design.

The truth is that tools won't make your organization fit any more than a new pair of track spikes would have made me fast. Don't get me wrong—I loved buying new racing spikes, but they didn't make any difference on the stopwatch (sadly). The past 25 years have provided ample evidence that tools alone are insufficient. You can look up how to make a *heijunka* board; you can read a book on setting up a *kanban* system; you can hire a consultant to set up manufacturing cells; and in the end, you'll join the very long list of companies that attempted to copy Toyota's tools and ended up mired in mediocrity. There is a place for tools, of course, but they're useless unless they're deployed in an environment that honors the fundamental principles I've described in this book.

Implementing these principles will set you on the road to organizational fitness. And as with personal fitness, the biggest obstacle is likely to be . . . you. Your own well-established habits and preferences, your likes and dislikes, your own inertia will be a challenge to overcome. Getting out of bed at 5 a.m. in the middle of winter for a swim workout or an eight-mile run isn't easy, and neither is coaching a frontline worker through yet another problem-solving session when you'd rather just tell him what to do.

Culture's no excuse, either. Yes, you'll undoubtedly face some resistance to the changes you want to make. However, it's likely that the resistance is largely due to fear from past experiences with command-and-control leaders or the cynicism of dealing with managerial "flavor of the month" initiatives. That resistance will dissipate when people hear the sincerity of your words and witness the commitment of your actions. Think about the excitement of the nurse manager who said, "When I realized that improvement was about saving time, making our work easier, and improving patient care, I realized that I had a lot of ideas after all!" Or imagine the powerful feeling of shared destiny at FastCap, where Paul Akers spends time on the production line stuffing parts in bags and the three people on that line came up with a better improvement than he did. Cultural resistance fades quickly in an environment where process improvement and employee development are built into the fabric of daily work. Those reactions are a major part of the joy of building and leading a fit organization.

Whether you're a Fortune 500 company or a five-person organization that doesn't even subscribe to *Fortune*, you can embark on this fitness program. It's simple (if not easy), and progress will be slow. But the financial, intellectual, and emotional rewards make it a journey worth taking.

W. Edwards Deming said, "Survival is optional. No one has to change." He was right, of course, but that doesn't mean that it has to be a long slog through the muck under enemy fire. It can be a path filled with challenge and even, as Menlo Innovations shows, joy.

The choice is yours.

APPENDIX 1
Organizational Fitness
Self-Assessment

As you know, I didn't give you any specific tools in this book. I'm also not providing a self-assessment that gives you some sort of arbitrary score. I'm not sure that there's any value to finding out that you scored a 58, or a 73, or an 88—are those scores good or bad? And what should you do next?

Instead, I've constructed a self-assessment that will force you to think and reflect on how you and your organization currently operate with respect to the six principles I've identified. If your organization is large, you may need help in answering some of the questions. That's fine. Think of this as a learning tool that will identify areas of strength and weakness and help you to focus your fitness efforts in the future.

COMMITTING TO FITNESS

Do you have a clearly stated goal of continuous improvement for individual processes and operations within the company?

☐ Yes   ☐ No

How do you measure improvement?

_____

_____

_____

How does your organization view problems—as opportunities for improvement, or as obstacles to work around?

☐ Opportunities   ☐ Obstacles

How do you recognize and reward small improvements when people create them?

_____

_____

_____

Do you teach scientific thinking (Plan-Do-Study-Adjust) and problem solving?

☐ Yes   ☐ No

What process do you use to teach PDSA thinking?

_____

_____

_____

Do you personally participate in improvement activities?

☐ Yes   ☐ No

Do you give people time each day and week for improvement?

☐ Yes   ☐ No

How do you solicit employee ideas for improvement?

_____

_____

_____

How quickly do supervisors/managers/executives respond to employee suggestions?

☐ Within 2 days
☐ Within 1 week
☐ Whenever we get around to it
☐ Never

How often do you implement employee ideas?
☐ We always find something to implement
☐ More than 80 percent of the time
☐ About 50 percent of the time
☐ Less than 25 percent of the time
☐ Never

INCREASING VALUE, NOT CUTTING COSTS

Aside from period-end financial statements, what measurements do you use to assess your organization's operations?

_____

_____

_____

What internal metrics do you currently track?

_____

_____

_____

When faced with financial downturns, what other initiatives besides cost-cutting do you pursue?

_____

_____

_____

THINKING HORIZONTALLY

What are your major customer groups or types?

_____

_____

_____

How do you measure how well you're serving these customer groups? (What measurements do you have for customer satisfaction?)

_____

_____

_____

Do you have ideas or input from customers about what other products or services, or improvements in current products or services, they would like from you?

☐ Yes   ☐ No

What are they?

_____

_____

_____

What systems or processes do you have to provide different types of service for each customer type?

_____

_____

_____

Standard Work

Do all jobs in the company have documented, up-to-date, easy-to-use standard work?

_____

_____

_____

Who creates the standard work?

_____

_____

_____

Do leaders have standard work that is clearly visible and known to all?

_____

_____

_____

How often do leaders adhere to their standard work?

_____

_____

_____

How often do leaders go to the front lines of the company as part of their regular work (i.e., not for some sort of emergency)?

☐ Every day
☐ Most days
☐ Seldom
☐ Almost never

Visual Management

Which processes in your organization have visual controls?

_____

_____

_____

Are these visual controls used regularly and updated frequently, or are they obsolete decorations?

☐ Used and updated
☐ Decorations

Do these visual controls indicate quality of work?

☐ Yes   ☐ No

Do these visual controls indicate whether the process is ahead or behind?

☐ Yes   ☐ No

Do these visual controls show what stage the work is in (i.e., where it is in the process)?

☐ Yes   ☐ No

COACHING

How often does your leadership team coach employees?

☐ Every day
☐ Most days
☐ Seldom
☐ Almost never

What is the substance of the coaching—job-specific skills or more general skills (e.g., communication, public speaking, Excel, etc.)?

_____

_____

_____

How often does middle management coach frontline workers?

☐ Every day
☐ Most days
☐ Seldom
☐ Almost never

What is the substance of the coaching—job-specific skills or more general skills (e.g., communication, public speaking, Excel, etc.)?

_____

_____

_____

Do you coach on problem solving/scientific thinking?

☐ Yes   ☐ No

Do you coach in your office or where the person works?

☐ My office
☐ Where the person works

What are the standard questions that you ask the person being coached?

_____

_____

_____

How do you evaluate the progress of the person being coached?

_____

_____

_____

Appendix 2
Resources

I've held off from sharing specific tools with you until this final appendix for a reason: deploying tools without embracing the underlying principles is a waste of time, effort, and money.

Take the case of General Motors. In the 1990s, it attempted to use the remarkable performance at NUMMI, its joint venture with Toyota, to improve its other plants. A VP ordered a lower-level manager to make his plant look *exactly* like the NUMMI plant by taking photos and copying every square inch of the factory. Not surprisingly, the attempt failed miserably, because the manager could only copy the tools, not the underlying principles. The most egregious example of this misunderstanding was the "andon" cord. At NUMMI, pulling this cord allowed any worker to stop the production line in order to fix a quality or safety problem. Pulling the cord was not only permitted, it was a requirement of the job—quality and process improvement was everyone's responsibility. But at the other GM plant, workers who pulled the andon cord were criticized for slowing down production. The plant manager was evaluated on the number of cars that rolled off the line each day, regardless of quality, and he wasn't going to allow a young worker concerned about a scratch in a car's paint to mess with his bonus. The andon cord went unused, quality didn't improve, and it was business as usual. Tools are insufficient. It's the underlying philosophy that matters. (And that, by the way, is why Toyota is happy to let competitors go on factory tours at the company. Copying visible tools is trivial. Copying the philosophy is colossally difficult.)

However: Once you've understood and committed to the underlying principles, there are tools that will support your own organizational fitness program. Here are a few of them.

A3 THINKING

As I argued in Chapter 1, scientific thinking through the PDSA cycle is the foundation of improvement. There are a variety of methods that teach PDSA, but I'm partial to the A3 approach. A3s (named for the international paper size—approximately equal to 11-by-17-inch ledger paper—that you write on) provide a concise and elegant method of working through the four phases of problem solving. Warning: the A3 is deceptively difficult. The single-page format looks easy to complete, but it masks the hard work that underpins a robust problem-solving effort. When it's done well, the A3 identifies root causes, suggests a suite of countermeasures, provides a way of evaluating success, and creates alignment around the course of action you want to take. These two books will help you understand and use this tool well:

> John Shook, *Managing to Learn: Using the A3 Management Process to Solve Problems, Gain Agreement, Mentor, and Lead* (Lean Enterprise Institute, 2008). This book does double duty, teaching the reader both how to engage in structured PDSA thinking and how to coach people effectively. The book tracks the process by which a young employee learns

how to use an A3 to solve a particularly complex problem and how his supervisor/mentor challenges and teaches him how to think scientifically. The protagonist's educational journey mirrors the reader's, making it a powerful and compelling story.

Durward Sobek and Art Smalley, *Understanding A3 Thinking: A Critical Component of Toyota's PDCA Management System* (Productivity Press, 2008). Sobek and Smalley's book is a deep dive into the specifics of the A3. It's the one book you need to deploy scientific problem solving in your organization.

VALUE STREAM MAPPING

A value stream is all the actions required to deliver a product or service to an internal or external customer. Value stream mapping makes the invisible flows of work and information through these streams visible. Mapping brings everyone involved in a process together to discuss how things *actually* operate in the organization, using nothing more than markers, Post-it Notes, and wide sheets of paper. Once you have a clear understanding of the current state, you can create a future state version that depicts visually how you want to improve the process by increasing the value delivered to the customer. The mapping activity is so powerful because it provides a deeper understanding of the problems within processes and generates alignment around potential improvements. Value stream maps are often embedded within A3s as part of understanding the current conditions, and they can also spawn A3s if they reveal complex problems that need to be solved. Here are three of the best books on the subject:

Mike Rother and John Shook, *Learning to See: Value Stream Mapping to Add Value and Eliminate MUDA*

(Lean Enterprise Institute, 1999). More a workbook than a textbook, this book takes the reader through the development of current state and future state maps for the fictional Acme Stamping company.

Karen Martin and Mike Osterling, *Metric-Based Process Mapping: Identifying and Eliminating Waste in Office and Service Processes* (Productivity Press, 2012). This book shows how to use the concepts from *Learning to See* in the office and service environments. It also provides useful templates and a detailed, step-by-step method for conducting the mapping exercise.

Karen Martin and Mike Osterling, *Value Stream Mapping: How to Visualize Work and Align Leadership for Organizational Transformation* (McGraw-Hill, 2013). This book provides a higher-level view of mapping. It shows how to work with larger sections of a value stream rather than the nitty-gritty operational details and discusses the managerial and organizational benefits of the exercise.

VISUAL MANAGEMENT

Visual management systems form a language that captures and displays the essential elements of your current operational system. They're more than just a tracking device. When designed and implemented skillfully, they allow you to see how processes operate; they make manifest how you think about your customer; they highlight information deficits and gaps in daily operations; and they shine a spotlight on the gap between where you are and where you want to be. From this perspective, creating visual controls is itself a powerful method of attaining alignment and clarity around objectives and values. Your own imagination and creativity are the only limitations.

Gwendolyn Galsworth, *Visual Systems* (AMACOM, 1997). Galsworth has written *the* book (many books, actually) on creating visual controls in the workplace. She covers both the principles and the practices of visual systems, and her examples cover the gamut of issues important to helping you assess processes in real time, including safety, quality, and fundamental information deficits.

STANDARD WORK

If you're committed to implementing standard work, you need to go back to the origins in Training Within Industry. As I explained earlier, standard work is, in many ways, the foundation for improvement: if you don't have a baseline, you can't tell if you've changed for the better. But the benefits go beyond that. If you implement it properly, it's a collaborative effort among leaders and frontline workers that pays dividends in terms of both process improvement (quality, safety, and cost) as well as the development of critical thinking and analytical skills.

Donald Dinero, *Training Within Industry: The Foundation of Lean* (Productivity Press, 2005). *TWI* is the bible for both creating standard work and—just as important—teaching it to workers quickly and effectively. Although TWI is most often used in manufacturing settings, the lessons in this book will help you bring it and its benefits to the office and service environments.

Daniel Markovitz, *A Factory of One: Applying Lean Principles to Banish Waste and Improve Your Personal Performance* (Productivity Press, 2012). My first book touches on the application of lean concepts to individual knowledge work. Although I'm inclined to think that all the points are indispensable (naturally!), I believe that the section on standard work is particularly valuable for leaders. Even though the leader's job is fundamentally chaotic, there are ways to deploy standard work and reap the benefits.

Coaching

I've argued that coaching is (or should be) the primary function of leadership. Unfortunately, most leaders have never gotten coaching on how to coach. Even if they were lucky enough to have a great mentor during their career, it's likely that the mentor never made the subtle elements of effective coaching explicit. Understanding the coaching dynamic and learning how to avoid the most common coaching errors (e.g., giving instructions rather than asking questions, or providing answers instead of setting goals) is essential to developing and increasing the innate capabilities of your employees.

> Mike Rother, *Toyota Kata: Managing People for Improvement, Adaptiveness, and Superior Results* (McGraw-Hill, 2009). Rother's book delivers a clear explanation of the theory behind effective coaching and its role in continuous improvement. Perhaps even more important, he provides a concrete, step-by-step playbook for both the coach *and* the learner. Even if you haven't been fortunate enough to have been taught how to coach, the Improvement Kata and the Coaching Kata will jump-start the process for both leaders and frontline workers.

> Michael Ballé and Freddy Ballé, *Lead with Respect: A Novel of Lean Practice* (Lean Enterprise Institute, 2014). The latest in the Ballés' series of business novels shows what coaching looks and feels like in daily conversation between a boss and her employees, and between a customer and his vendor.

What's particularly noteworthy is the way the conversations embody respect, both in the conventional sense (not being a bully or a jerk) and in the continuous improvement sense (continual pushing and challenging for better performance). It's not a how-to guide, but rather the gestalt of respectful coaching.

Read these books, learn the skills, understand the concepts—they'll take you far. But first, make sure that you've embraced the principles I've discussed in this book. The last thing you need is another shelf of expensive books gathering dust because the ideas can't take root and flower in your organization. But if you combine the six principles with these powerful tools, nothing can stop you and your organization from attaining greatness.

Notes

CHAPTER 1

1. James Surowiecki, "Better All the Time," *New Yorker*, November 10, 2014.
2. "The Big Picture: HDTV and High-Resolution Systems," *Congress of the United States Office of Technology Assessment*, Appendix A, 92.
3. Barnaby J. Feder, "Last U.S. TV Maker Will Sell Control to Koreans," *New York Times*, July 18, 1995.
4. "Detroit Is Finally Closing the Car Quality Gap with Japan," Associated Press, February 21, 2012, via Business Insider, http://www.businessinsider.com/detroit-is-finally-closing-the-car-quality-gap-with-japan-2012-2.
5. Paul Akers, *2014 Lean Year End Message* video, https://www.youtube.com/watch?v=_pidcXnnkfk.
6. W. Edwards Deming, *Out of the Crisis* (Cambridge: MIT Press, 1986), 202.
7. Kettering University, http://paws.kettering.edu//~jhuggins/humor/quotes.html, accessed January 30, 2015.
8. I'll explain PDSA in more detail later in this chapter.

9. Karen Martin, *The Outstanding Organization* (New York: McGraw Hill, 2012), 192–193.

10. *Hubie Brown on Jordan*, Michael Jordan Career Retrospective, National Basketball Association, http://www.nba.com/jordan/hubieonjordan.html, accessed January 30, 2015.

11. Taiichi Ohno, "Ask 'Why' Five Times About Every Matter," Toyota Global website, http://www.toyota-global.com/company/toyota_traditions/quality/mar_apr_2006.html, accessed January 30, 2015.

12. John Shook, "How to Change a Culture: Lessons from NUUMI," *MIT Sloan Management Review*, Winter 2010.

13. Carolyn Aiken and Scott Keller, "The Irrational Side of Change Management," McKinsey & Company, http://www.mckinsey.com/insights/organization/the_irrational_side_of_change_management.

14. Teresa Amabile and Steven J. Kramer, "The Power of Small Wins," *Harvard Business Review*, May 2011, https://hbr.org/2011/05/the-power-of-small-wins/.

15. Michael Ballé, "Products, People, Profits," *Industrial Engineer*, October 2014.

16. See Mark's KaiNexus webinars here: http://info.kainexus.com/webinar-download-leadership-behaviors, accessed February 2, 2015.

CHAPTER 2

1. John A. Byrne, "Chainsaw Al," *Bloomberg Businessweek*, October 18, 1999, http://www.businessweek.com/1999/99_42/b3651099.htm.

2. Tara Parker Pope, "The Fat Trap," *New York Times*, December 28, 2011.

3. Suzanne Heywood, Dennis Layton, and Risto Penttinen, "A Better Way to Cut Costs," *McKinsey Quarterly*, October 2009.

4. "Fit for Growth Index Profiler," reported in Strategy& press release, June 17, 2014, www.strategyand.pwc.com/ fit-for-growth-index-profiler.

5. Suzanne P. Nimocks, Robert L. Rosiello, and Oliver Wright, "Managing Overhead Costs," *McKinsey Quarterly*, May 2005.

6. Mark Graban, "The Little Difference That Turned 'No Ideas' Into 'Lots of Ideas,'" https://www.linkedin.com/pulse/ little-difference-turned-ideas-lots-mark-graban.

CHAPTER 3

1. A concise summary of this story is available at the Lean Voices blog: http://leanvoices.com/the-case-of-fujitsu-services-sense-and-respond-book-citation-by-bernard-marr/. More comprehensive treatments of the Fujitsu approach are available in Bernard Marr and Andy Neely's Cranfield University case study (https:// dspace.lib.cranfield.ac.uk/bitstream/.../callcentreperformance .pdf), and in Susan Barlow, Stephen Parry, and Mike Faulkner's book, *Sense and Respond* (Palgrave Macmillan, 2005).

2. Allen C. Ward and Durward K. Sobek, *Lean Product and Process Development* (Cambridge, MA: Lean Enterprise Institute, 2014), 51.

3. I've provided just a tiny window into the remarkable work Menlo Innovations is doing. Read the full story in Rich's book, *Joy, Inc.* (New York: Penguin Portfolio, 2013).

4. A "value stream" is the series of steps required to create, produce, and deliver a product or service to a customer. All organizations have value streams that serve external customers

(e.g., cancer, trauma, and psychiatry value streams in a hospital; cleaning products, beauty products, and baby products value streams in a consumer packaged goods company), and value streams that serve internal customers (for example, hiring and onboarding, facilities, and IT).

CHAPTER 4

1. Greg Bishop, "Tom Cruising," *Sports Illustrated*, December 15, 2014, 88.
2. James Surowiecki, "Better All the Time," *New Yorker*, November 10, 2014.
3. Kevin Starr, *Embattled Dreams: California in War and Peace, 1940–1950* (Oxford University Press, 2003), 129.
4. All statistics from the Wisconsin Manufacturing Extension Partnership, http://bit.ly/1A8TDex, accessed December 1, 2014.
5. Marc Onetto, "When Toyota Met E-Commerce: Lean at Amazon," *McKinsey Quarterly*, February 2014.
6. M. L. Emiliani, "Standardized Work for Executive Leadership," *Leadership and Organization Development Journal* 29, no. 1 (2008): 24–46.
7. Atul Gawande, "The Checklist," *New Yorker*, December 10, 2007.
8. Dan Heath and Chip Heath, "Heroic Checklist," *Fast Company*, February 14, 2008.
9. Paul Akers, *Lean Year End Message 2014*, YouTube video, https://www.youtube.com/watch?v=_pidcXnnkfk.
10. Gallup, *State of the Global Workplace*, available for download at http://www.gallup.com/services/178517/state-global-workplace.aspx.

11. See Greenleaf's essay, *The Servant as Leader*, for more information on this subject (https://www.leadershiparlington .org/pdf/TheServantasLeader.pdf).

12. Shai Danziger, Jonathan Levav, and Liora Avnaim-Pesso, "Extraneous Factors in Judicial Decisions," *Proceedings of the National Academy of Sciences*108, no. 17 (April 26, 2011).

13. Michael Lewis, "In Meetings, on the Court to Discover 'Obama's Way,'" *Fresh Air* interview, September 12, 2012.

14. Peggy Orenstein, "Stop Your Search Engines," *New York Times*, October 23, 2009.

CHAPTER 5

1. Micheline Maynard, "'The GM Nod' and Other Cultural Flaws Exposed by the Ignition Defect Report," *Forbes*, June 5, 2014.

2. Michael Ballé, *Lead with Respect* (Cambridge, MA: Lean Enterprise Institute, 2014), 34.

3. In 1999, NASA's Mars Climate Orbiter—cost for the hardware: $125 million; cost for the overall mission: $327 million—burned up as it began orbital insertion around Mars. The propulsion system overheated because the spacecraft dipped too deeply into the planet's atmosphere. The story that made the headlines was that the error was due to a mismatch between imperial units and metric units: the Lockheed Martin engineering team used imperial units, NASA used metric, and someone failed to make the (very simple) conversion. Oops. After a full investigation, Carolyn Griner, retired deputy director of NASA Marshall Space Flight Center, said that a simple, *unanswered* email about the correct measurement units

with no follow-up resulted in the missed orbit. This is the story that *should* have made the headlines. (From a speech delivered at the American Institute of Aeronautics and Astronautics, St. Louis Section, March 2001 dinner meeting.)

CHAPTER 6

1. Geoff Colvin, *Talent Is Overrated* (New York: Penguin Books, 2008), 134–5.
2. The concept of the four stages of competence or skill development is a mainstay of psychological theory. Developed by Noel Burch in the 1970s, it argues that people don't know what they don't know when they begin to acquire a skill. Once they advance enough to recognize their limitations, they practice their skills until they attain a level of competence. Finally, they can use the new skill without even thinking— becoming unconsciously competent. If you've ever taught a teenager how to drive (to say nothing of parking) a car, you're probably painfully aware of these stages.
3. Atul Gawande, "Personal Best," *New Yorker*, October 3, 2011.
4. Charles Fishman, "No Satisfaction at Toyota," *Fast Company*, December 2006/January 2007.
5. Ben Shpigel, "Thanks to a Cerebral Influence, the Lions Find Enlightenment," *New York Times*, December 20, 2014.
6. "The Toyota Way," *White Coat Black Art* interview, CBC Radio, October 17, 2014, http://www.cbc.ca/player/Radio/White+Coat+Black+Art/Full+Episodes/ID/2559937050/.
7. Ken Iverson, *Plain Talk* (New York: John Wiley & Sons, 1998), 55.
8. Barry Wehmiller website, http://www.barrywehmiller.com/our-culture.

9. Jacob Stoller, *The Lean CEO* (New York: McGraw-Hill, 2015), 169–170.

10. *Ibid*, 172.

11. Christine Porath and Christine Pearson, "The Price of Incivility," *Harvard Business Review*, January 2013.

12. Gawande, "Personal Best."

13. Mike Rother, *Toyota Kata* (McGraw-Hill: New York, 2009).

Index

About the Author

Daniel Markovitz is president of Markovitz Consulting, a firm that helps organizations become faster, stronger, and more agile through the application of lean principles to knowledge work. He has worked with nonprofit and governmental organizations such as the New York City Department of Health, Sutter Health, and Memorial Sloan Kettering Cancer Center, as well as a diverse roster of corporations such Starkey Technologies, W. L. Gore & Associates, Abbott Vascular, Clif Bar, Hydro Flask, and CamelBak.

An internationally recognized speaker, he has keynoted conferences and delivered seminars at the Lean Summit (U.K.), the Lean Island Conference (Iceland), the Lean Transformation Summit (U.S.), the Rome Confluence Conference, the Outdoor Industry Association Rendezvous, the Printing Industry Association Continuous Improvement Conference, and numerous Association for Manufacturing Excellence conferences. Dan is a faculty member at the Lean Enterprise Institute and teaches regularly at the Stanford University Continuing Studies program. He also lectures at the Ohio State University Fisher School of Business.

Dan's first book, *A Factory of One*, was honored with a Shingo Research Award in 2013. He has also published articles in the *Harvard Business Review* blog, *Quality Progress*, *Industry Week*, *Reliable Plant*, and *Management Services Journal*, among other magazines.

Dan lived in Japan for four years and is fluent in Japanese. He received his BA from Wesleyan University and his MBA from the Stanford Graduate School of Business.